THE ART OF THE BOOK IN THE TWENTIETH CENTURY

JERRY KELLY

The Art of the Book
in the Twentieth Century

A STUDY OF ELEVEN INFLUENTIAL BOOK

DESIGNERS FROM 1900 TO 2000

RIT CARY GRAPHIC ARTS PRESS

ROCHESTER, NEW YORK

MMXI

LIBRARY OF CONGRESS CATALOGING-IN-PUBLICATION DATA

Kelly, Jerry, 1955-
   The art of the book in the twentieth century : a study of eleven influential book
designers from 1900 to 2000 / Jerry Kelly.
      p. cm.
   Includes bibliographical references.
   ISBN 978-1-933360-46-1 (alk. paper)
1. Book design--History--20th century. 2. Book designers--Biography. 3. Type
designers--Biography. 4. Printers--Biography. I. Title.
   Z246.K45 2010
   686.09'04--dc22

                                                                      2010019785

Published and distributed by:

RIT CARY
GRAPHIC ARTS
PRESS

RIT Cary Graphic Arts Press
90 Lomb Memorial Drive · Rochester, New York 14623-5604
http://carypress.rit.edu

ISBN 978-1-933360-46-1

TABLE OF CONTENTS

Introduction — VII

Daniel Berkeley Updike — 24 FEBRUARY 1860–31 DECEMBER 1941 — 3

Bruce Rogers — 14 MAY 1870–18 MAY 1957 — 19

Joseph Blumenthal — 4 OCTOBER 1897–4 JULY 1990 — 37

Stanley Morison — 6 MAY 1889–12 OCTOBER 1967 — 55

Francis Meynell — 12 MAY 1891–10 JULY 1975 — 71

Giovanni Mardersteig — 8 JANUARY 1892–27 DECEMBER 1977 — 85

Jan van Krimpen — 12 JANUARY 1892–20 OCTOBER 1958 — 101

Jan Tschichold — 2 APRIL 1902–11 AUGUST 1974 — 115

Max Caflisch — 25 OCTOBER 1916–3 MARCH 2004 — 129

Gotthard de Beauclair — 24 JULY 1907–31 MARCH 1992 — 141

Hermann Zapf — 8 NOVEMBER 1918– — 157

Bibliography — 172

Index — 175

INTRODUCTION

The twentieth century was a time of phenomenal change. At the beginning of the century, air travel, television, skyscrapers, and mass production were unheard of, to say nothing of computers, plastics, etc. By the end of the century these were all commonplace. Their effect on our lives and psyches has yet to be fully determined.

In the arts also, the years between 1900 and 1999 saw radical changes: at the beginning of the century classical realist painters such as Thomas Eakins and John Singer Sargent were the best known in America; by the end of the century non-representational painters such as Jackson Pollock and Richard Diebenkorn were familiar names. The more practical arts, such as industrial design and architecture, also developed from a classically inspired symmetrical style practiced by McKim, Mead, and White, to a clean, simpler style with little reference to the Greek or Roman ages, as in the work of Frank Lloyd Wright, Marcel Breuer, and Mies van der Rohe.

There is no reason that book design, while a most circumscribed art, should not display a similar degree of change. At the beginning of the century, an historically inspired classicism prevailed (as seen in the work of Rogers, Updike, Meynell, and others), while at the end of the century a more modern, simpler, open style predominated – a style which intentionally rejected backward-looking classicism based on the revival of earlier typefaces, ornaments, and other design elements. This change came not only from a shift in aesthetic principles (which can also be seen in other arts throughout the century), but also from a radical shift in production methods which inevitably affect design principles. It is true of any art or craft that as the method of manufacture changes, the aesthetic principles involved in design will adapt to best reflect (and indeed exploit) the potential of the new processes. With the twentieth century being a time of such significant change in manufacturing procedures of all kinds, it follows that design principles would evolve simultaneously– or at least following closely on the tail of – new methods of production.

How did book production methods change between 1900 and 1999? It would be easier to enumerate how book production remained static in that period. Only binding retained some of the basics of nineteenth-century manufacture, and even in this instance, one could cite significant changes. In 1899 virtually all typesetting was done in metal, and a large proportion of that was hand composition, whereby an individual would typeset words by picking individual letters out of a typecase and assembling them in proper order (though keyboard typesetting via the Linotype and Monotype machines had been making inroads in typesetting since the 1890s – albeit still using cast metal letters). In the interim, a period of phototypesetting – computer input paired with output via light, film, and photosensitive paper – had come and gone. By 1999 more than ninety-nine percent of type was computer input and digitally output on a laser device.

Metal type had to be printed by letterpress – whereby a raised surface was inked and then impressed on paper, like a woodcut or linoleum cut (or even a potato print). In 1900 nearly ninety-nine percent of all books were printed in this manner. By 1999 more than ninety percent were printed by offset lithography, a process in which a printing plate with a photosensitive coating is exposed to light through film. This plate is then put on a press where – based on the principle that oil and water do not mix – ink adheres to the exposed areas of the plate, while the other areas repel the greasy ink. The ink is then transferred to another "offset" cylinder which makes contact with the paper to receive the image.

Photo and digital-type generation allows for a greater degree of freedom in type design. For example, long overhanging parts of letters (such as on an italic f or a long-tailed capital Q, called "kerns" in metal type) are difficult and impractical to manufacture in metal type, but it is no problem to include such characters in digital type fonts. Offset printing also offers a wider range of possibilities to the designer: large solid areas are little problem for offset, even when fine-line type is dropped out to white, something which is extremely difficult to do in letterpress. Fine-line screens which can reproduce a wide range of tones for illustrations – or be used to "gray-down" type or solid areas – were little trouble for offset printing by the end of the century. Again, this was impractical for letterpress printing. Designers could incorporate these new features into their typography and design, along with the evolving aesthetic principles which invariably occur with the march of time.

Even at the very beginning of the twentieth century, newer technologies gave book designers options that were unavailable in the preceding centuries. Photo reproduction techniques developed in the late 1800s allowed designers to copy just about any line image from the past on metal printing plates for letterpress. Before that time images had to be hand cut into either wood or metal and then printed by letterpress (analogous to the way metal type is printed) or intaglio (which uses an incised line that is much finer than a relief line, but which had to be printed separately from type). Mechanical typesetting machines using a keyboard for inputting text – as opposed to tedious and uneconomical hand setting – led to a proliferation of typefaces that offered a range of fonts to the typographer, undreamed of in centuries past. Skillful designers used these early twentieth-century technologies to produce stunning designs in period style, arranging early type designs in modern re-cuttings along with historical decoration to produce some truly beautiful books. While such pastiches of earlier layouts could not have been achieved without the newer technological innovations just described, the question arose whether such design principles were true to the twentieth century. Was it "good" to copy a fine fifteenth-century type such as Jenson and mix it with a handsome re-drawing of a sixteenth-century initial and headband, as Bruce Rogers did in *The Centaur*? Could it truly be a masterpiece of bookmaking when new castings of some of the earliest extant type fonts (the so-called Fell types from the seventeenth century) were combined with old-fashioned ornaments in a thoroughly archaic style, as Francis Meynell did in his Nonesuch Press edition of John Donne's *Paradoxes and Problemes* (figure 2)? Would it be better to use a twentieth-century type with a living artist's woodcuts, as the same designer did in his edition of *Genesis*, or as Joseph Blumenthal did in his edition of *Aesop's Fables* with woodcuts by Antonio Frasconi (figure 3)? Or would it be more appropriate to print an unornamented text in a strikingly modern typeface,

FIGURE 1

Maurice de Guérin, *The Centaur*, privately printed, 1915. Typography by Bruce Rogers. Typeface based on a fifteenth-century Italian model combined with decorations based on sixteenth-century French books.

THE CENTAUR. WRITTEN BY MAURICE DE GUERIN AND NOW TRANSLATED FROM THE FRENCH BY GEORGE B. IVES.

I Was born in a cavern of these mountains. Like the river in yonder valley, whose first drops flow from some cliff that weeps in a deep grotto, the first moments of my life sped amidst the shadows of a secluded retreat, nor vexed its silence. As our mothers draw near their term, they retire to the caves, and in the innermost recesses of the wildest of them all, where the darkness is most dense, they bring forth, uncomplaining, offspring as silent as themselves. Their strength-giving milk enables us to endure without weakness or dubious struggles the first difficulties of life; yet we leave our caverns later than you your cradles. The reason is that there is a tradition amongst us that the early days of life must be secluded and guarded, as days engrossed by the gods.

My growth ran almost its entire course in the darkness where I was born. The innermost depths of my home were so far within the bowels of the mountain, that I should not have known in which direction the opening lay, had it not been that the winds at times blew in and caused a sudden coolness and confusion. Sometimes, too, my mother returned, bringing with her the perfume of the valleys, or dripping wet from the streams to which she resorted.

Now, these her home-comings, although they told me naught of the valleys or streams, yet, being attended by emanations therefrom, disturbed my thoughts, and I wandered about, all agitated, amidst my darkness. 'What,' I would say to myself, 'are these places to which my mother goes and what power reigns there which sum-

breaking many of the conventions of symmetrical typography along the way, as Jan Tschichold would do in the many volumes he designed before his conversion to classical principles around 1940? (pp. 132–45) These were the questions that vexed the finest book designers of the twentieth century. The best of these designers would never produce a didactic copy of an earlier printed book (though they may occasionally come pretty close). Instead, through their adaptation of an earlier format, and their skill in the arrangement and execution of their volumes, they would produce an exceptional work which was a new and imaginative creation in its own right. The same can be said of the radical new thinkers, who would employ fresh resources in a unique ways to produce completely original works; this, too, often resulted in masterpieces of book design, as examples on the following pages will attest. Indeed, in many instances may be found examples from both schools of thought in the work of one designer. I have already mentioned two very different examples from the work of Francis Meynell in this regard (see also the chapter on Jan Tschichold, who turned from radical modernist to devoted classicist during his career spanning the half-century from 1920 to 1970).

The question of whether the lifting of an early design to create a new work is a valid artistic method, or rather more a copy than an inspired reinterpretation, is a subtle one. In 1923 Francis Meynell copied a border originally used by Jean de Tournes for

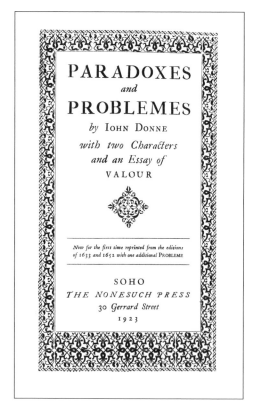

FIGURE 2

John Donne, *Paradoxes and Problemes,* London: The Nonesuch Press, 1923. Typography by Francis Meynell. Type and ornaments from the seventeenth century, arranged in an appropriate manner.

The Hare with Ability and
the Tortoise with Staying Power

A lively young hare and an old tortoise lived near a
racetrack, and the hare teased the tortoise; and one day,
when the horses were running somewhere else, and
they had the place to themselves, they engaged in a race.
The hare, calculating how long it was going to take his

adversary, confident in his streamlined figure and
powerful hind legs, got bored and sleepy, and decided
to take time out for a nap. He overslept. Meanwhile
the tortoise crept along in front of the grand-stand,
slow but indefatigable and victorious.
Persistent ambition without talent breaks no record.
Talent without character wins no race.

FIGURE 3   Antonio Frasconi (illustrator), *Twelve Fables of Aesop*. New York: Museum of Modern
Art, 1954. Typography by Joseph Blumenthal. Modern layout using a twentieth-century typeface
(Blumenthal's Emerson font).

his 1556 edition of the works of Louise Labé (figure 6). Meynell arranged the typography within the border in a manner similar to de Tournes' original layout,
using relatively heavy caps for the first line of the title, followed by smaller sizes of
type in a symmetrical pyramid arrangement, just as de Tournes had done (figure 4).
He even used a small star ornament, as de Tournes did centuries earlier. The same
border was copied by Bruce Rogers for his 1903 edition of the *Songs and Sonnets of
Pierre de Ronsard* (figure 5). But here Rogers used the border to totally different effect: he spliced an additional section into the design to make for a longer and narrow-
er proportion. For the typography within the border, Rogers created a novel arrangement of all caps with some swash characters in one size only, justified left and right,
creating a tight block of letters. The result is very different from the pages of de
Tournes and Meynell; and the Ronsard title page can be considered a twentieth-century masterpiece. But one can also find examples of more didactic copying in Rogers's
œuvre: for his 1923 edition of *The Journal of Madam Knight* (figure 8) Rogers
adapted quite directly the typography of *A Journey from Aleppo to Jerusalem*, a
1703 volume published by the Oxford University Press (figure 7). Rogers even went

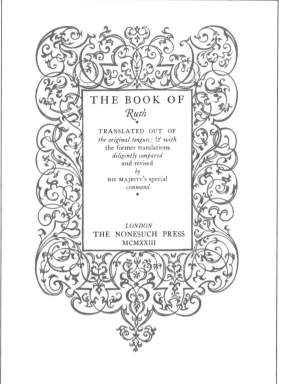

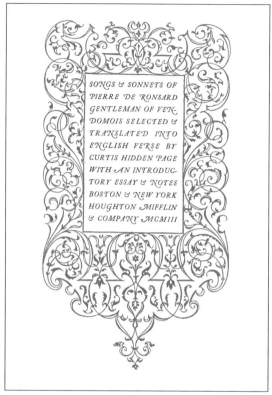

FIGURE 4 *The Book of Ruth*. London: The None-such Press, 1923. Typography by Francis Meynell.

FIGURE 5 *Songs & Sonnets of Pierre de Ron-sard*. Cambridge: Riverside Press editions, 1903. Typography by Bruce Rogers.

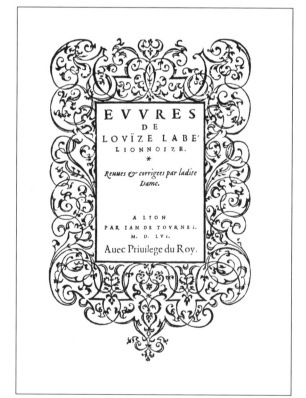

FIGURE 6

Oeuvres by Louise Labé. Printed by Jean de Tournes, 1556. This sixteenth-century border was the basis for the two twentieth-century borders shown above.

so far as to use an upside-down "n" in a much larger font size in the word "Journal" on his title page to accurately mimic the unusual form of U from the font used in the word "Journey" on the Oxford page. The Oxford University Press book was set in one of the more eccentric sizes from the fonts brought to the Press in the seventeenth century by Bishop Fell. Yet in other instances, such as the magnificent *Fra Luca de Pacioli* designed by Rogers for The Grolier Club in 1933 (figure 10), he would take earlier designs and use them in new ways, creating a fresh work from an assortment of materials based on earlier sources, in this case the *Summa de Arithmetica* printed in Venice in 1494 (figure 9).

For some book designers, there was no use for earlier design models in modern typography. Various graphic artists such as Merle Armitage, W. A. Dwiggins, and especially proponents of the Bauhaus style such as Herbert Bayer and the young Jan Tschichold, totally eschewed revivals of earlier typefaces, decorations, and layouts. These typographers used mostly contemporary typefaces with no historical precedent, arranged in novel ways for twentieth-century books. Many manifestoes professing the appropriateness of modern materials and the folly of copying earlier de-

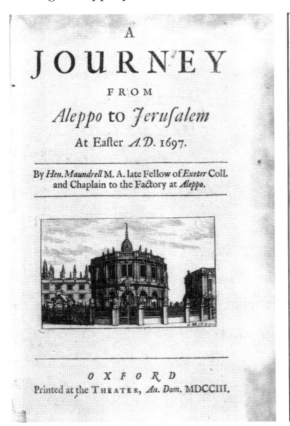

FIGURE 7 *A Journey from Aleppo to Jerusalem.* Oxford University Press, 1703.

FIGURE 8 *The Journal of Madam Knight.* Boston: Small, Maynard & Company, 1920. Typography by Bruce Rogers. Note upside-down "n" in "Journal" showing the extent to which Rogers would mimic the volume at left.

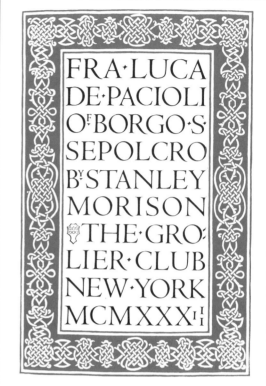

FIGURE 9 Fra Luca de Pacioli, *Summa de Arith-metica*, Venice, 1494.

FIGURE 10 Stanley Morison, *Fra Luca de Pacioli.* New York: The Grolier Club, 1933. Typography by Bruce Rogers.

signs were published. Dogma ruled, yet it is interesting to note how frequently these advocates violated their own dicta. Again, the example of Jan Tschichold, who did a complete about-face from asymmetric typography to severely classical design based on historical models, is pivotal in this regard.

Others have shown the possibilities of using modern types which are not historical revivals, but still in the classical vein. Jan van Krimpen designed original typefaces not based directly on any earlier model (as his friend Stanley Morison was doing at the British Monotype Corporation), but also not radically different from the letter-forms which have become the norm for the Roman alphabet. He used his own types (and others) in classical, symmetrical arrangements that were of their time, yet essentially unchanged from the tenets which tradition had established. Giovanni Mardersteig used both his own classically inspired type designs and historical revivals in a totally classical manner, producing some of the most sought-after fine editions of the century on his hand press, the Officina Bodoni. Four of Mardersteig's proprietary type designs (Griffo, Zeno, Fontana, and Pacioli Titling) were based on historical models, but his last design (Dante), while inspired by renaissance forms, is an original font in the classical style.

There did evolve, however, something of a middle ground. For designers such as Joseph Blumenthal, Gotthard de Beauclair, Hermann Zapf, and Max Caflisch, the line was not so firmly drawn between designs based on historical precedents and fresh, new arrangements using materials and layouts not seen prior to the twentieth century. In their work one can find a mixture of historical adaptations and novel designs. While allusive typographers such as Daniel Berkeley Updike and Meynell, as well as modern classicists such as Van Krimpen and Mardersteig rarely, if ever, used a sans serif font, Caflisch, de Beauclair, and Blumenthal would not hesitate to employ one when they deemed it appropriate. Blumenthal was a generation younger than his countrymen Updike and Rogers, and his work shows a tendency towards more modern elements. Allusive typography and historical type revivals abound in the book designs of Rogers, Updike, and Morison – and examples of such styles can be readily found in the work of Tschichold and others – but more often a newer, modern aesthetic is shown in the work of the latter designers. Whereas Updike and Rogers most often based the decoration in their books on historical models, Blumenthal preferred commissioning contemporary artists to produce modern decorations and illustrations. He also used quite a few then-new typefaces (such as Koch Antiqua, Bernhard, Futura, and his own excellent Emerson font) in more modern

FIGURE 11

Jan Tschichold, *Asymmetric Typography*. New York: Reinhold Publishing, 1967. Typography by the author. A thoroughly modern design for this dust jacket.

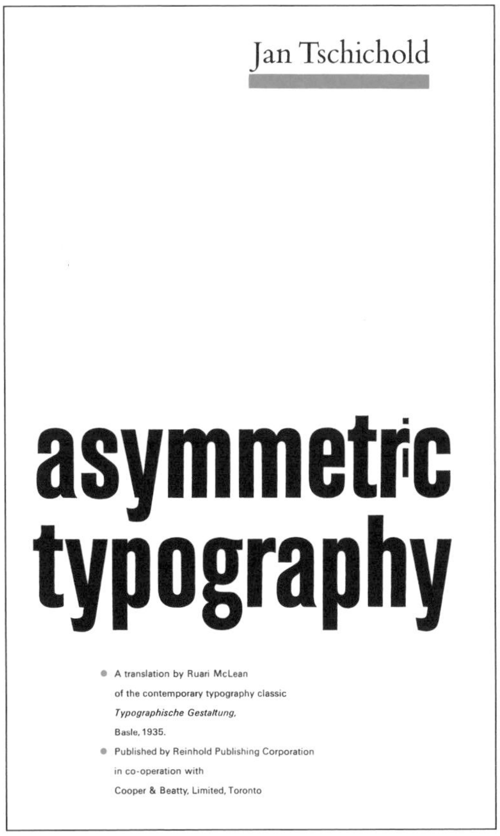

Jan Tschichold

asymmetric typography

● A translation by Ruari McLean
of the contemporary typography classic
Typographische Gestaltung,
Basle, 1935.
● Published by Reinhold Publishing Corporation
in co-operation with
Cooper & Beatty, Limited, Toronto

JOHN DONNE

POEMS

SELECTED FROM HIS

SONGS AND SONETS

ELEGIES

EPITHALAMIONS

VERSE LETTERS

DIVINE POEMS

AMSTERDAM
A. A. BALKEMA
1946

FIGURE 12

John Donne, *Poems*. Amsterdam: A. A. Balkema, 1946. Typography by Jan van Krimpen, using his Romulus typeface in a clean, clear arrangement. Modern – but by no means avant-garde.

arrangements. Younger typographers, such as Kim Merker, Gotthard de Beauclair and Hermann Zapf were to develop this modern – yet not radical – style even further, preferring original contemporary typefaces (which were not necessarily sans serif or radically divergent from the classical norm), and arranging the type in a clear, open manner – sometimes symmetrically, sometimes asymmetrically, but always logically and clearly, in a fresh way. In addition, contemporary materials (such as machine-made papers, offset printing in addition to letterpress, and machine typesetting – including digital character generation) were exploited to their best advantage by these master typographers. The result is a modern style of book design that could never be mistaken for a pastiche of earlier styles, but which also does not reject the tenets of legibility, clarity, and fitness for use that have been proved valid through half a millennium of book typography.

Overall there are some common denominators throughout the work of talented book designers, whether they be severely classical and historical-minded, or modern and avant-garde. It has been said that the proper disposition of type on a page, where leading, typesize, spacing, and other variables are artistically considered, creates a visual image that is in itself a unique graphic art, unlike any other. This holds true for carefully designed pages employing all typefaces and styles, whether sans serif or

serif, historical revival or totally original designs, asymmetrically arranged or justified, etc. All great book design is built around the single element of a fine type page;
headings, title page, binding, and other aspects of the book's design follow from that.
In all the work that follows, the type page has been carefully considered. Extraordinary care has been taken by these typographers to combine the proper leading, typeface, spacing, paper, impression, and other factors to create that elusive object: a
pleasing page of type.

The care in the spacing of typography – as well as ornament and illustration, if any
is used – can be meticulous. It would surprise many a layman to know how painstak-
ingly some designers have adjusted the space around parentheses or dashes; or
struggled with hanging punctuation in the margin; to say nothing of the careful
spacing of letters in a typeface, especially when it comes to lines set all in capitals.
With a large amount of intensive study one might be able to recognize the work of
a particular designer just by the way a line of caps is spaced (since each designer will
see the spacing slightly differently), just as one might recognize the subtle nuances
of a particular musician or draftsman.

Much of book design is the selection of materials. Paper (including text, endpapers,
and any other paper used in the volume), binding materials, type and ornaments,
even small details such as headbands are all carefully selected by fine book designers. Sometimes an unusual source is used for unusual materials, such as specially
woven fabric, exotic papers, or long-forgotten typefaces or decoration. In the hands
of a master book designer, such items can yield surprisingly attractive results, when
used tastefully.

Within these parameters, an infinite amount of variation is possible. Book designers
in the twentieth century have explored myriad styles and possibilities, while using
technological advances to their advantage in creating a plethora of styles – from allusive historicisms and restrained classicism to novel and unprecedented designs.
The following pages will attest to the vitality and triumphant skill displayed by
some modern masters of the art of the book through their arrangement of the various elements involved in book design.

Unfortunately reproductions, no matter how carefully produced, can only partially
convey the effect of a finely produced book: we cannot reproduce the paper it was
printed on, nor create a facsimile of the particular impression of type on that paper,
to say nothing of binding designs and materials, or even elements as basic as the size,
heft, and overall "feel" of a particular volume (all characteristics which are carefully considered in fine printing). We can only reproduce (a generation removed) the
graphic image on the paper. Interested readers should seek the opportunity to see the

work as a whole in libraries or collections, with the information discussed in these pages as a guide.

*

The purpose of this book is not to document all the movements from 1900 to 1999 in the small world of book design, nor is it to highlight the greatest masters of the craft for that period. Instead, it is meant to give an introduction to the work of eleven of the most important practitioners of book design in the twentieth century, albeit briefly. The selection – both of the designers and of their works – is somewhat arbitrary, but through the text and the hundred or so plates, a beginning can be established for further study of the art of book typography in the twentieth century – a century which saw so much change and variety in the field. Often a selection was made to avoid repeating an oft-reproduced page, or to illustrate a specific point in the text, rather than to show the most successful examples or a complete survey of that particular designer's work.

The work of many excellent designers has been left out of this brief sampling, but this is in no way meant to reflect the relative merits of practitioners of book design. Instead, a small sampling has been selected to display some of the range and evolution of the art of the book from 1900 to 1999, a most remarkable period in the history of the art of the printed book.

THE ART OF THE BOOK IN THE TWENTIETH CENTURY

DANIEL BERKELEY UPDIKE

Daniel Berkeley Updike was born in Providence, Rhode Island, on 24 February 1860. In 1877, his father died, throwing the aristocratic and well-connected Updike family into a precarious position. While the death of the patriarch meant that the family felt they did not have the means to send young Daniel to college, their social connections were to serve him well all his life. However, his youth was spent in less than comfortable circumstances, requiring him to seek employment at a young age.

One of the family's friends secured a position for Updike as an errand boy at Houghton Mifflin & Company, the Boston publishers, in 1880. Eventually he was entrusted with some work of a typographic nature – mainly advertisements for the firm – along with a small sprinkling of book work. In order to better understand the process with which he was becoming more deeply involved, namely typography, Updike was transferred to Houghton Mifflin's printing operation, The Riverside Press. Houghton Mifflin was a prospering publisher, so the printing division was well-equipped and the work flow was steady, providing fertile ground for a budding printer. Indeed, the same fertile environment was soon to sprout another of America's great typographers, Bruce Rogers, who, ten years Updike's junior, was to start at Riverside in 1893, a couple of years after Updike left.

Updike's first major independent book project was the decoration of *The Book of Common Prayer* of 1892. Later, in 1928, he would produce a masterpiece by printing the revised edition of the same title. It was an unusual assignment: the book had already been set in type and printed by the De Vinne Press in New York in 1892, and Updike was retained to add ornamental borders and complete the project, which was then issued in 1893. The production was financed by J. P. Morgan. Another early commission was *The Altar Book*, begun in 1892 and completed in 1896. The project was backed by Harold Brown, a family connection and a good friend of Updike's, who earlier had collaborated with him on (and financed) the *Dedication of American Churches*, printed at the Riverside Press in 1891.

The Book of Common Prayer of 1892, like much of Updike's early work as an independent designer/printer, was in the Morris-Kelmscott Press mold, from which Updike would eventually move away (see, for example, one of the first Merrymount Press announcements, printed in Morris style with blackletter type, red side headings, with an old-looking line illustration, plate 1). However, the influence of Morris and the Arts and Crafts movement stayed with him for many years, as can be seen quite clearly in the 1896 *Altar Book*, which Updike designed with more complete control than the 1892 *Book of Common Prayer*.

The 1896 *Altar Book* displays one of the hallmarks of many of Updike's important books: the close collaboration with a carefully selected and closely directed group of artists in the production of suitable ornament and decoration. For this volume Updike commissioned illustrations from Robert Anning Bell, together with borders and a new typeface from Bertram Grosvenor Goodhue.

Updike was employed at The Riverside Press from 1880 to 1892. He started as an office boy but by the end of his time there, had graduated to typographic work. Updike became convinced that he must strike out on his own. In 1892, the large commission to print the *Altar Book* gave him the impetus to start The Merrymount Press. For several years the "press" consisted only of typesetting equipment with no printing machinery, but in 1903 three presses were added to the operation.

The somewhat melancholic Updike often underrated his own achievement. He did, however, acknowledge how printing as a vocation changed the course of his life. In 1927, with over three decades of impressive work behind him, and with many important books still to be printed at his Press, Updike summed up his life this way:

> Starting with no education, not much health, little money, and a generally poor and impractical training for life, and being pushed by necessity into printing, a work that I hated, by studying that work and persistently keeping at it, I have succeeded better than some men, and, in spite of many handicaps, made myself over through it.

Updike has often been noted as having broken new ground in maintaining the standards of a fine press while sustaining a viable commercial printing operation. Indeed, this was unique for his day. By comparison, the great university presses may have been well within the tradition of fine printing, but they were often subsidized operations; a plant such as The Riverside Press was a captive shop which did not necessarily have to heed the vagaries of the marketplace. Updike established a press which did work consistently on a par with the best while surviving in the often harsh world of free enterprise.

The ability to make ends meet at The Merrymount Press had a great deal to do with the business acumen of John Bianchi, who was employed at the Press from its earliest days, becoming a full partner in 1915. Updike benefitted from several fortunate connections with wealthy patrons. In 1900, Updike's close friend Harold Brown left him $25,000 – a very tidy sum of money in those days. As we have seen, Brown also financed the printing of *On the Dedication of Churches* and *The Altar Book*. J. P. Morgan, Jr. sponsored the 1928 *Book of Common Prayer* (plate 9), the billing of which totaled over $60,000, even though Morgan and his librarian Belle da Costa Greene balked at the expense of installing humidifying equipment needed for printing the twelve copies on vellum.

Updike displayed almost uncanny foresight in his selection of artists early on in their careers. He commissioned work from W. A. Dwiggins, T. M. Cleland, and Rudolph Ruzicka in the very first years of the twentieth century, quite early in the careers of each of these artists. One suspects Updike's overseeing of these young people was substantial, since often the final art is more recognizable as the work of Updike than the artist himself! Who could see the mature Dwiggins style in the title page for the Humanists' Library *Petrarch* (plate 5), or in the initials for the second *Book of Common Prayer* that Updike was to work on (dated on the title page 1928, the year the text was completed, but not finished until 1930, the year stated in the colophon). What sign is there of the typical rococo style of Cleland in his ornaments for the Merrymount *Rossetti*?

Perhaps Rudolf Ruzicka more than any other artist, developed a mature style which is consistently associated with The Merrymount Press. Ruzicka first met Updike in 1907, when he was just twenty-four and had been an artist in New York City for four years. Ruzicka and Updike remained close friends and business associates until the latter's death in 1941. In addition to illustrating many of The Merrymount Press's finest books (for example, *Newark* [plate 3] and the charming three-volume Washington Irving), Ruzicka created color woodcuts of various Boston locations as an annual New Year's keepsake from the Press, and the Press in turn did much of Ruzicka's printing.

Updike equipped The Merrymount Press with relatively few fonts of type, but the ones he did install were meticulously chosen, and some of the faces such as Janson (as seen in *The Book of Common Prayer* of 1928 and *Saint George's Chapel*) and Bell (called "Mountjoye" by Updike before its true origins were discovered), both acquired in 1903, were extremely rare at the time. He was the first printer in America to install Stanley Morison's Times New Roman type. In addition, two fonts were commissioned especially for the Press. While Updike himself used these proprietary Merrymount and Montallegro (plate 5) types with some success, neither can be said to be of enduring value.

What the Merrymount Press had in great quantity was an extensive resource of rare ornaments and decorative cuts, most of which are now in the Bancroft Library in California. It is notable that in the first announcement of the establishment of his independent work (1893), Updike refers to his typography as "decorative printing and book-making," terms he repeats again in a later announcement upon adopting the name "The Merrymount Press." Some of The Merrymount Press's diverse decorative material was used to very different effect in *Pierrot's Verses* (plate 4) and *Two Letters of Charles Lamb* (plate 2). Updike's taste in using appropriate ornamentation, often derived from earlier periods, in the right context for a vast array of printed matter – from fine books to ephemeral printing (plate 6) – is key to his success as a designer.

The Press was never a large operation, even though over a thousand books and almost twenty times as much ephemeral printing were produced there in a span of over fifty years. The maximum number of employees came to only thirty-five, including fifteen compositors (most of the books of the Press were handset, even though Monotype machines were installed later on), four pressmen, and two proofreaders. At Merrymount's height the staff operated three cylinder and two job presses. The Press occupied six locations from 1893 to 1949.

After a few years of flirting with the Morris /Arts and Crafts style, Updike drew inspiration from other more varied sources for his work. A strong Venetian influence can be seen in the Humanist's Library volumes (eight were published all told, plate 5), and the quintessential Updike style, if one is to be singled out – and a strong argument can be made against this when reviewing the entire varied output of this press – can be seen in such volumes as *Old Mrs. Chundle, Letters of Bulwer-Lytton to Macready* (1911, plate 7), and the magnum opus, *The Book of Common Prayer* of 1928 (plate 9). These books, as well as dozens of other Merrymount productions, show a strong eighteenth-century British influence. W.A. Dwiggins succinctly summed up Updike's mastery of typography as follows:

He manipulates space with the discrimination of a Renaissance architect. He designs with space and with the sizes and colors of type letters.

What unites all of Updike's work, whether from the early years of the Press or the wide variety of later styles, is an appropriateness to the subject, a strong adherence to the highest standards of workmanship and fine bookmaking, and tasteful and studied handling of type. Updike was prescient when he wrote in a letter in 1924:

I am certain that after the uproar has ceased over decoration and historical styles . . . we shall ultimately find that they are only fitted for work of a limited nature, and shall have to invent new types of a more modern feeling, or else use more colourless types which, since they do not reflect any particular period of their own, will be less "in the way of" the mind when we print works by modern authors.

One might ask, where does this substantial body of work stand in light of today's typography and fine bookmaking? Allusive typography, of which Updike was one of the earliest proponents, has been out of favor for decades. Much of the ornament and many of the types employed by The Merrymount Press are scarcely seen in today's books.

If one thread is common to all of the work of The Merrymount Press, however, it is a constant attainment of the highest quality in the minute yet important details that go into fine bookmaking. The grain of the paper almost always runs in the proper direction, the care in typesetting and the presswork were always superlative, with a tasteful combining of all elements in an attractive yet never jarring manner. Even the most mundane volume or piece of ephemera – for instance a small institution's annual report or a program for a conference (both of which were printed by The Merrymount Press) – that may have been given up as insignificant, were printed in a manner which fine presses around the world today can still hold up as a model. One will never find a poorly positioned title page, or misplaced copyright line in a Merrymount book, but all too often today, an otherwise well-produced book is marred by such a glaring defect. This overall care in the production of a book or piece of ephemera followed through into the choice of appropriate paper, proofreading, binding. In short, no detail essential to the production of a piece of printing was ever slighted. Stanley Morison recounted this achievement in 1947, in a memorial article after Updike's death on 31 December 1941, as follows:

The essential qualities of the work of The Merrymount Press, i.e. accurate composition of text; occasional decoration; proportionate and therefore satisfactory imposition; scrupulous presswork; careful folding, sewing and wrapping of finished product, may be said without exaggeration . . . to have reached a higher degree of quality and consistency than any other printing-house of its size, and period of operation, in America or Europe.

As we have said, Updike broke new ground in establishing a commercially-based fine printing establishment. In this regard, he served as a model for many fine presses that followed, including The Printing House of William Edwin Rudge (where Bruce Rogers produced many exceptional books), The Spiral Press, and The Stamperia Valdonega. Before Updike set his example, the line was firmly drawn between the fine presses such as the Kelmscott, Doves, and Village Presses, and the larger commercial houses working to a different standard. Even those few shops which could at times attain the level of craftsmanship of fine printing – such as the Chiswick or De Vinne Presses – did not always see such an extreme amount of care as mandatory for all the kinds of printing which a commercial printing house must handle.

In addition, Updike was one of the preeminent scholar-printers of the twentieth century. Through numerous books and articles, he contributed much to the art which provided him with a livelihood. His essays on printing are known far and wide, and his monumental two-volume work, *Printing Types* (first published in 1922), was seminal in its day and is still an essential reference for typographic scholarship. While much has been added to our knowledge since its publication, *Printing Types* covers an enormous amount of material with a good deal of depth. The beginning and ending sections contain gems of typographic wisdom which hold as true today as ever, and we can predict that his generalizations in these chapters will remain forever pertinent to the printer's craft.

Updike's extensive study of the history of printing was not done solely for its own sake: it also informed every piece of his own typography to create what was then a contemporary style, not simply a rehashing of earlier layouts. No one said it better than Updike himself:

> Tradition must and does influence the modernist, if by tradition we mean patient and respectful appraisal of what that accumulation of yesterdays, which we call the past, has to teach. It is only by experience that we can effect a wise blend of the two. Then we produce books which, while representing the best practice of our time, will outlast it.

Updike was the continuation of a long line of scholar-printers, dating back to Aldus and continuing through Estienne and Plantin, through to Reed and De Vinne. This torch was nobly carried by Morison (who was greatly inspired by Updike), Mardersteig, and Blumenthal, among others.

Updike first became associated with book printing quite by accident in the spring of 1880 at Houghton Mifflin and Company. His years at the firm were spent across the river in Cambridge at The Riverside Press, the printing works of the publisher. His experience there would lay the groundwork for his great accomplishments at The Merrymount Press, which he founded in 1893.

A few years later, in 1896, a man from Indiana who was ten years Updike's junior would take up the position he had vacated at The Riverside Press. This young man would, in addition to continuing Updike's typographic chores, establish a fine printing department that would display a panache and diversity never before seen in book typography. That young man was Bruce Rogers. From 1896 to 1912 he would launch a career in typography that led him to be called by Francis Meynell "the greatest artificer of the book who ever lived."

PLATE 1 An early Merrymount Press promotional booklet.

Charles Lamb

A LETTER regarding Roast Pig to WILLIAM HAZLITT
and
A LETTER on Friendship to ROBERT LLOYD
together with
A DISSERTATION on ROAST PIG

Privately Printed for his Friends by
W. K. BIXBY
1922

PLATE 2 Decoration adapted from the nineteenth century.

NEWARK

A SERIES OF ENGRAVINGS ON WOOD BY

RUDOLPH RUZICKA

WITH AN APPRECIATION OF
THE PICTORIAL ASPECTS OF THE TOWN
BY WALTER PRICHARD EATON

THE CARTERET BOOK CLUB
NEWARK · NEW JERSEY
1917

PLATE 3 Caslon types (with an in-line added to the heavy Caslon capitals with a graver by Rudolph Ruzicka).

PIERROT'S VERSES

By Maria de Acosta Sargent

Privately Printed

MDCCCCXVII

PLATE 4 Derivative title-page with vignette by W. A. Dwiggins.

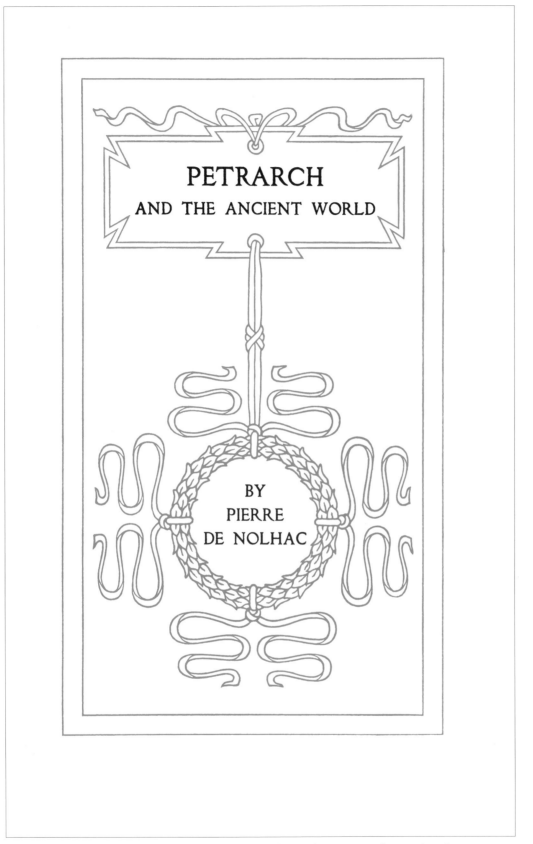

PETRARCH
AND THE ANCIENT WORLD

BY
PIERRE
DE NOLHAC

PLATE 5   Type (Montallegro) and ornamentation by Herbert Horne, designed under
D. B. Updike's direction.

Muſic & Dances
Colonial Entertainment at THE CHILTON CLUB,
At Ten O'Clock on the Evening of *New Year's* Day, 1920.

PROGRAMME

Gavotte

From " Paris and Helen," GLUCK
American String Quartette

Miſs *Gertrude Marſhall*	*Firſt Violin*
Miſs *Ruth Stickney*	*Second Violin*
Miſs *Edith Jewell*	*Viola*
Miſs *Hazel L'Africain*	*Violoncello*

Songs

" Verduron, Verduronette"	Arranged by *Weckerlin*
" A Paris, je sais trois filles "	Arranged by *Weckerlin*
" Le Petit Mari"	*Child's Song*
" O No, John!"	*Old Engliſh.* Arranged by *Cecil Sharp*

Miſs Marian Sprague

Minuet

Muſic by LUIGI BOCCHERINI
American String Quartette

Dancers

Mrs. *Robert Livermore*	Mr. *Newell Bent*
Mrs. *Ronald Lyman*	Mr. *George Foote*
Mrs. *Francis P. Sears*	Mr. *Cuſhing Goodhue*
Miſs *Miriam Sears*	Mr. *Harriſon Mifflin*

Songs

" The Heavy Hours"	Arranged by *Samuel Endicott*
" The Birds Courting"	Arranged by *Robert Hughes*
" Il était un oiseau gris"	*Monſigny*
" Ma fille, veux-tu un bouquet?"	*Old French Song*

Mrs. Daniel de Menocal

Tambourin: RAMEAU
American String Quartette

*The Spinet is loaned through the courteſy of Mr. STEINERT;
The Minuet was prepared by Miſs PAULINE JONES.*

PLATE 6 Printed ephemera from The Merrymount Press.

LETTERS

OF

BULWER-LYTTON TO MACREADY

WITH AN INTRODUCTION BY

BRANDER MATTHEWS

1836–1866

PRIVATELY PRINTED

THE CARTERET BOOK CLUB

NEWARK, NEW JERSEY

1911

PLATE 7 Title page in a nineteenth-century British style.

STEPHEN CRANE

BY

Thomas L. Raymond

NEWARK NEW JERSEY

The Carteret Book Club

1923

PLATE 8   An example of a less derivative approach by Updike.

THE BOOK OF COMMON PRAYER

and Administration of the Sacraments
and Other Rites and Ceremonies
of the Church

ACCORDING TO THE USE OF THE
PROTESTANT EPISCOPAL CHURCH
IN THE UNITED STATES OF AMERICA

Together with The Psalter
or Psalms of David

PRINTED FOR THE COMMISSION

A. D. MDCCCCXXVIII

PLATE 9   This edition of the revised *Book of Common Prayer* is considered Updike's masterpiece.

PHOTO BY HOWARD COSTER

BRUCE ROGERS

Bruce Rogers was born in Lafayette, Indiana, on 14 May 1870. He was gifted with a fine ability as a draughtsman, a skill which he would put to good use in his long career as a book designer. Unlike Updike, Rogers drew almost all of his own ornaments, lettering, and decoration – rather than commissioning these services from others. He enrolled at Purdue University in 1886, majoring in art. He was one of only two male art majors in his class, the other being John McCutcheon, who would later gain fame as an illustrator. As a young man Rogers worked for a brief time as a landscape painter and a newspaper illustrator, but the turning point came for him in the early 1890s when Joseph M. Bowles (who ran an art store in Indianapolis) showed him a few of the books printed by William Morris at his Kelmscott Press (whose first publication appeared in 1891). Immediately upon seeing the Kelmscott books, with their handmade paper, strong, historically derived typefaces with matching decorative initials and borders, and full vellum or holland-backed blue boards bindings, Rogers was "hooked." From then on, he would devote his efforts to the design and ornamentation of books – preferably fine books, but occasionally a superior "regular" edition.

Bowles was also involved in publishing. He started a magazine called *Modern Art* in 1893, and printed a related book every so often. In both endeavors he secured the assistance of Rogers. A few other publishers benefitted from Rogers's nascent efforts, including Way & Williams in Chicago and Thomas Bird Mosher of Portland, Maine; the real breakthrough was to come after the young Rogers joined Houghton, Mifflin & Co. at The Riverside Press in Cambridge, Massachusetts.

Early in his career at Houghton Mifflin (from 1896 to 1900) Rogers tilled much the same soil as his predecessor, Daniel Berkeley Updike. After a few years, he became more interested in producing fine editions – using better papers, finer bindings, and with more time and funds available for developing special typography and ornamentation. Eventually (after going so far as threatening to quit), Rogers was given the opportunity to establish a department of special printing at Riverside. There, over the next dozen years, through sixty special Riverside Press Editions, as well as hundreds of trade books for Houghton Mifflin, he would make typographic history. While the concern for materials, craftsmanship, and history instilled by the Kelmscott example were inspirational to The Riverside Press Editions (see plate 11), the general aesthetic was different. Rather than applying a heavy, uniform style, using only one or two typefaces, papers, and binding styles, Rogers saw each new volume as an opportunity to explore a different typographic style related to the origin and text of the piece being printed. Each title would evoke a strong sense of a specific time: *Petrarch's Sonnets* was adorned with renaissance woodcut-style decoration; Ronsard's poems (figure 5, Introduction) were printed with a lovely adaptation of a Jean de Tournes border from the sixteenth century; the *Symposium* was austere and completely unadorned, eliciting a classical simplicity for the text by Plato; Lowell's *Democracy* was set in a bold, almost crude early-American style; and so on. This style (or styles) of designing with a layout that refers – or alludes – to an appropriate earlier look is called "allusive typography." Both Updike and Rogers were to practice this technique to great acclaim in the United States (as did Morison and Meynell later in England). But none of these designers were content to produce a sterile copy of an earlier typographic style. Instead, typefaces, decorations, and other elements were adapted, revised, and changed in various ways to produce an original work, albeit clearly harking back to a recognizable prior era. Occasionally each of these typographers designed a book which was completely fresh, or even consciously modern, with no earlier precedent, but the overwhelming bulk of their output was based on allusive typography.

At their finest, such as Rogers's edition of *Fra Luca de Pacioli* (figure 10, Introduction) with a scholarly text written by another great twentieth-century book designer, Stanley Morison, for The Grolier Club (1933), or the beautiful privately printed edition of Homer's *Odyssey* (translated by T. E. Lawrence, also known as Lawrence of Arabia, plate 19), Rogers's volumes transcend whatever elements refer to an earlier time, and become new, vibrant works in themselves, while incorporating appropriate references to historical styles. In a few other books, such as the monumental lectern *Bible* designed by Rogers for the Oxford University Press (1935) or the 1940 edition of *The Wind in the Willows* printed for The Limited Editions Club, a modern style is successfully achieved, without any reference to earlier times. Still, Rogers's work is most recognizable as a skillful and beautiful adaptation of an appropriate earlier typographic style.

In many ways the variety, skill, and joyous experimentation of his Riverside era was never surpassed by Rogers, though one cannot overlook the masterpieces from later in his career: books such as the Homer and Bible referred to above, and others such as *Of the Just Shaping of Letters* by Dürer (one of his earliest editions away from Riverside, 1915, plate 14); *Aesop's Fables* (The Limited Editions Club, 1933); *Utopia* (also for The Limited Editions Club, 1934, plate 18); *The Boswell Papers* (privately printed, issued in eighteen volumes from 1929 through 1933); the edition of Euclid's *Elements of Geometry, Book I* (plate 20) published by Random House (1944); and the *Complete Poems of Robert Frost* (The Limited Editions Club, 1950) – among many, many others – are superlative examples of the printer's art.

Upon leaving Riverside, Rogers dabbled in designing books at several presses. This included Norman T. A. Munder in Baltimore, Carl Rollins's press in Montague, Massachusetts (where Rogers would print the first book in his important new typeface, *The Centaur* [figure 1, Introduction]), and Emery Walker's works in London, England, before settling down to a more or less steady free-lancing existence at the Press of William Edwin Rudge in Mount Vernon, New York, where he was active from 1920 to 1928.

Rudge's shop employed the finest materials available at the time, including machine composition in both Monotype and Linotype, in addition to a wide range of handset foundry typefaces. Rudge maintained a very high standard in presswork and composition, with the noted expert Edith Diehl running the bindery. He also gave Rogers all the leeway he wanted in producing his commissions to the highest level. Many exceptional works were produced by Rogers at Mount Vernon, and these publications employed a wide array of types which Rudge made available for his use. Notable publications from this period are *The Journal of Madam Knight* (1920, figure 8) using the recently cut Garamond of American Type Founders, *The Pierrot of the Minute* (1923) in handset Deberny type with charming Fournier ornaments printed in a rose-red; *The Construction of Roman Letters* (1924) in Rogers's own Centaur type (here used with an alternate lowercase "e"), the first specimen of Frederic W. Goudy's Italian Old Style for the Monotype Corporation (1924, plate 16); *Ancient Books and Modern Discoveries* (1927, in Van Krimpen's Lutetia with a few alternate characters); and *The Psalms of David* (1928) in Linotype Granjon.

Rogers was a restless spirit, and by the late twenties he again longed to work in England, where he lived from 1916 to 1919. He always felt that England was more conducive to the kind of work he wanted to do. In 1928, at the age of 58, having an admirable lifetime of achievement in the design of fine editions behind him, Rogers sailed across the Atlantic in the hope of making books which he felt would more greatly fulfill his potential. Indeed, the printing of at least three masterpieces (the *Odyssey*, *Pacioli*, and *Bible*) during the period he spent in England (1928 to 1935) would prove to be the crowning achievement of a long and illustrious career.

In 1935, Rogers returned to the United States, where, at an age when many people settle into retirement, more than two decades of productive work lay ahead for him. Rogers established ties with some of the finest printers in the northeastern United States, including The Press of A. Colish and Marchbanks Press in New York, and later the new firm of Clarke & Way (Rogers was instrumental in bringing Bert Clarke and David Way together for this partnership). Again, many fine books issued from Rogers's designs, including the Euclid and Frost already mentioned, as well as The

Limited Editions Club's Shakespeare in thirty-nine volumes (1939–1940); the small, charming edition of Joseph Conrad's short story "The Tremolino" (1942); and the handsome edition of the *Twelve Moneths* printed by Clarke & Way in 1951. This book and others from the late period use sumptuous handmade paper. For example, see also the Rowfant Club's edition of Dard Hunter's early autobiography, *Before Life Began,* printed on paper handmade by Hunter at his Mill in Lime Rock, Connecticut. Rogers was often afforded the opportunity to employ unusual types or as many colors as he pleased, as in *The Twelve Moneths,* but somehow these later volumes never quite achieve the adventurous delight of The Riverside Press Editions, nor the sophisticated achievement of Rogers's major works from the late twenties and thirties. Still, the several dozen books designed by Rogers after 1935 would have been a major achievement for most other typographers. Rogers died on 18 May 1957, just after his eighty-seventh birthday.

When Rogers began his career, the private presses were doing the greatest work in the field of finely printed editions, usually with a quite distinctive and rather circumscribed look. Rogers took the best tenets of Kelmscott, Doves, Ashendene, Cranach, and others, and expanded them into a multi-faceted design repertoire that proved extremely successful. He felt most appreciated in England, where several of that nation's finest typographers practiced a Rogers / Updike-like style of allusive typography. While many of his books were striking and perhaps more "outgoing" than the subtle designs of some of his contemporaries, Rogers always kept the dictums of fine book design in mind. Several times he strove for a simple, relatively modest volume that would not be limited to the shelves of collectors, such as with the Cambridge edition of *Euclid in the Greek,* or the seven titles printed in his Hesperides series. All told, Rogers's output assures him a place among "the immortals of the book," as Joseph Blumenthal so aptly put it.

*

Rogers's achievements were much feted in his lifetime – and after. Numerous publications have appeared on the work of this great American book designer. The most thorough account of his life and career can be found in the 1989 biography entitled *Bruce Rogers: A Life in Letters, 1870–1957,* written by another printer, Joseph Blumenthal. Blumenthal, an exceptionally fine practitioner of book design, held Rogers in the highest esteem, and yet it is interesting to note how different an aesthetic Blumenthal displayed at his Spiral Press.

PLATE 10   One of the charming Riverside Press editions.

VI

And that for/gevyn is hir weked dede;
Than shal they come in/to that blysful place,
To whiche to comyn God synden us grace!'
The day gan failen, and the derke nyght,
That revith bestis from here besynesse,
Berafte me myn bok for lak of lyght,
And to my bed I gan me for to dresse,
Fulfyld of thought and busy hevynesse;
For bothe I hadde thynge that I nolde.
And ek I ne hadde thynge that I wolde.

But fynally, myn spirit at the laste,
For/wery of myn labour al the day,
Toke reste, that made me to slepe faste;
And in myn slepe I mette, as that I lay,
How Affrican ryght in the same a/ray
That Scipion hym say by/fore that tyde
Was come and stod right at myn bedis syde.

The wery huntere, sleppynge in his bed,
To wode a/gen his mynde goth a/non;
The juge dremyth how hise pleis been sped;
The cartere dremyth how his carte is gon;
The riche of gold; the knyght fyght with his fon;
The syke met he drynkyth of the tunne;
The lovere met he hath his lady wonne.

I can nat seyn if that the cause were
For I hadde red of Affrican by/foren,
That made me to mete that he stod theere,
But thus seyde he: 'Thow hast the so wel born
In lokynge of myn olde bok to torn,

PLATE 11 Text page from a Riverside Press edition set in Kelmscott-like blackletter style.

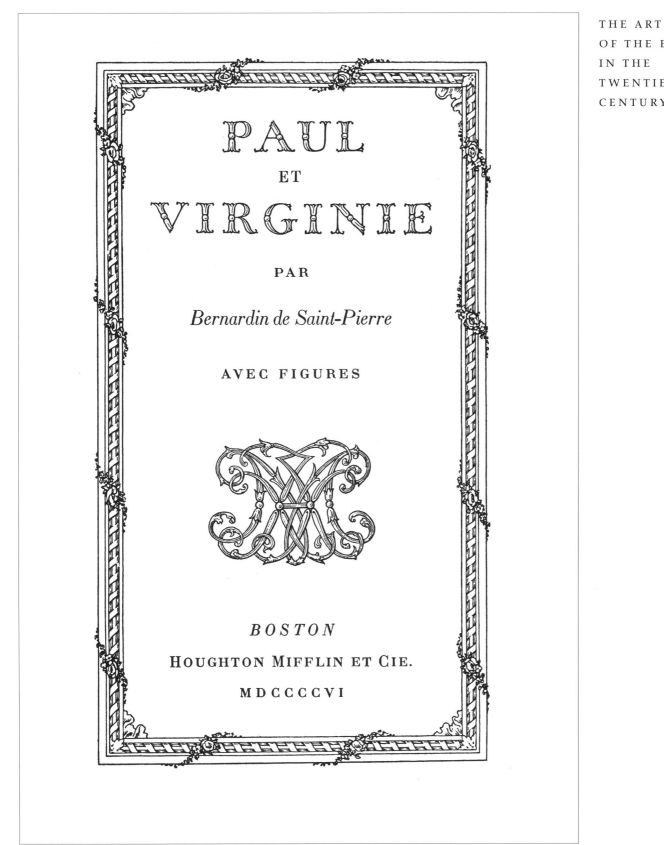

PLATE 12 Another Riverside Press edition, designed by Bruce Rogers in a manner totally different than those in the previous illustrations.

PLATE 13

Text spread from
The Riverside Press
edition of
Ecclesiastes, with
ornamentation
copied from
Geoffroy Tory.

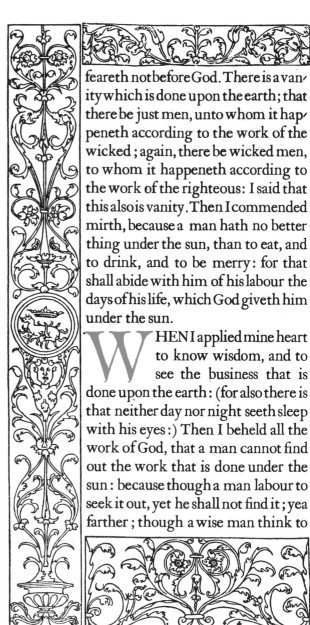

feareth not before God. There is a vanity which is done upon the earth; that there be just men, unto whom it happeneth according to the work of the wicked; again, there be wicked men, to whom it happeneth according to the work of the righteous: I said that this also is vanity. Then I commended mirth, because a man hath no better thing under the sun, than to eat, and to drink, and to be merry: for that shall abide with him of his labour the days of his life, which God giveth him under the sun.

WHEN I applied mine heart to know wisdom, and to see the business that is done upon the earth: (for also there is that neither day nor night seeth sleep with his eyes:) Then I beheld all the work of God, that a man cannot find out the work that is done under the sun: because though a man labour to seek it out, yet he shall not find it; yea farther; though a wise man think to

departeth in darkness, and his name shall be covered with darkness. Moreover he hath not seen the sun, nor known any thing : this hath more rest than the other.

YEA, though he live a thousand years twice told, yet hath he seen no good : do not all go to one place? All the labour of man is for his mouth, and yet the appetite is not filled. For what hath the wise more than the fool? what hath the poor, that knoweth to walk before the living?

BETTER is the sight of the eyes than the wandering of the desire; this is also vanity and vexation of spirit. That which hath been is named already, and it is known that it is man : neither may he contend with him that is mightier than he.

SEEING there be many things that increase vanity, what is man the better? For who knoweth

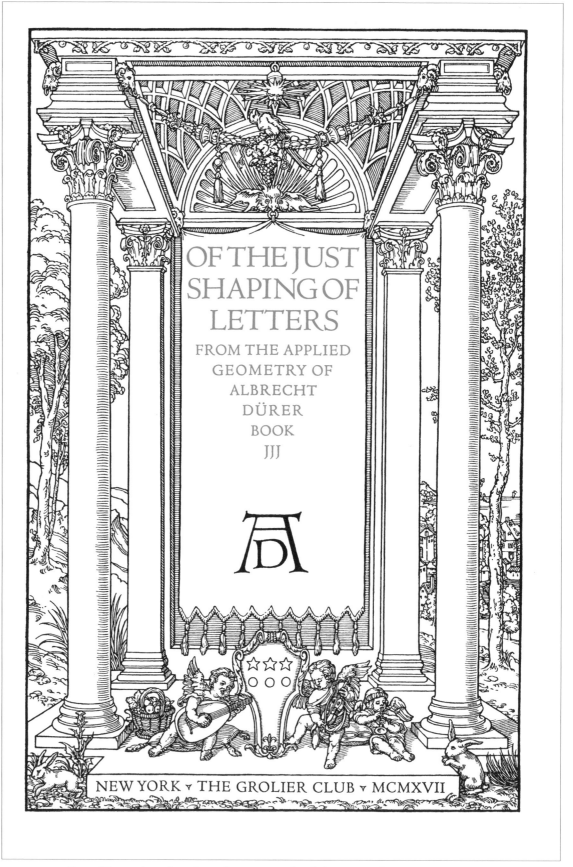

PLATE 14   One of Rogers's earliest fine editions outside of The Riverside Press.

28

48   CHAMP FLEURY

THE man in this figure, with feet and hands extended to equal dis-
tances, & the O, meet in the square, in the circle, and in the centre,
which betokens the perfection of the
human body & the said O, since the
circle is the most perfect of all figures
& the most comprehensive. The rec-
tangular figure is the most stable and
solid, especially when it is a cube, that
is to say, having six faces, like dice.

I Must not omit to show, by a figure
adapted to our said Attic letters,
how the man with arms extended &
standing erect on his feet, and having his centre, not in the navel, like
the last one drawn within the O, but in the groin, is a very clear demon-
stration of the way to know the precise spot to make the cross-stroke &
the joint (*briseure*) in the letters which require them—namely, A, B, E,
F, H, K, P, R, X, Y. For brevity's sake, I do not give a figure or example
of all of them, one after the other, but of three only—A, H, and K.

THE lower edge of the transverse
stroke of the letter A here drawn
is properly placed below the central
horizontal line of its square, & below
the groin of the man drawn therein.
All other letters which have a cross-
stroke or a joint have it above the said
horizontal line. But this letter A, because it is closed above & shaped like
a pyramid, requires its said transverse
stroke to be lower than the central
line. Thus this cross-stroke covers the man's organ of generation, to sig-
nify that Modesty and Chastity are required, before all else, in those
who seek acquaintance with well-shaped letters, of which A is the gate-
way and the first of all in alphabetical order.

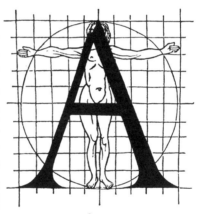

THE aspirate [H], then, has its cross-stroke on the central line, just
over the groin of the human body, to show us that our said Attic

PLATE 15   Text page for Geoffroy Tory's *Champ Fleury*, published by The Grolier Club in 1927.   29

PLATE 16 An exceptional original cover design by Rogers for the deluxe edition of the first specimen of
Frederic Goudy's Italian Oldstyle typeface.

PLATE 17   Unusual use of ornaments for a trade edition book published by Alfred A. Knopf.

UTOPIA
Written in Latin by
Sir Thomas More
and done into
English by
Ralph
Robynson

NEW YORK
THE LIMITED EDITIONS CLUB
1934

PLATE 18   Masterful use of type ornaments by Rogers.

BOOK XII

From Ocean's pouring stream our ship measured the open rolling seas even to Æaea, the isle of sunrise where Dawn the fore-runner has her house and dancing-floor: there we grounded the ship among the sand-banks and went out upon the beach, to sleep and wait for day. When the light came I sent a party up to Circe's house to bring down dead Elpenor's body. We hewed logs and built his pyre upon the tallest headland where it runs out above the sea: duly we made his funeral, bewailing him with bitter tears. After body and armour were quite burned away we piled a mound over them, and to crown it dragged up a monolith, on top of which we fixed his goodly oar. The busy work was scarcely done when Circe came, decked to receive us: our departure from Hades had not been hidden from her.

PLATE 19 *The Odyssey of Homer* (1932). Roundel in gold leaf in the original.

IV

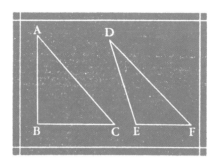

THEOREM: *If two triangles have two sides of the one equal to two sides of the other, each to each, and have also the angles contained by those sides equal to one another, they shall also have their bases or third sides equal; and the two triangles shall be equal, and their other angles shall be equal, each to each, namely those to which the equal sides are opposite.*

Let ABC, DEF be two triangles which have the two sides AB, AC equal to the two sides DE, DF, each to each, namely, AB to DE, and AC to DF, and the angle BAC equal to the angle EDF: the base BC shall be equal to the base EF, and the triangle ABC to the triangle DEF, and the other angles shall be equal, each to each, to which the equal sides are opposite, namely, the angle ABC to the angle DEF, and the angle ACB to the angle DFE.

PLATE 20 Euclid, *Elements of Geometry, Book One*. New York: Random House, 1944.

34

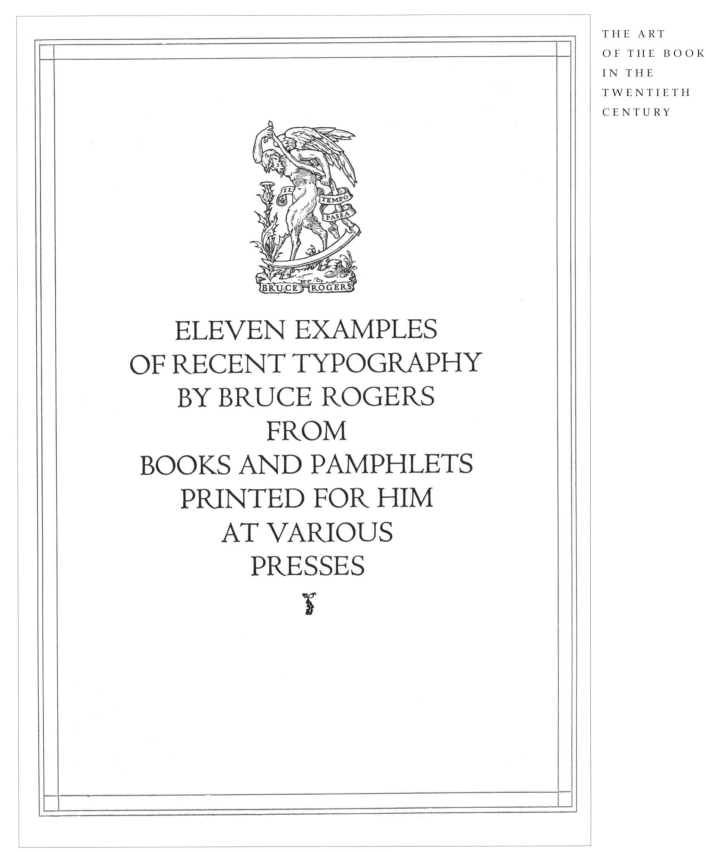

ELEVEN EXAMPLES
OF RECENT TYPOGRAPHY
BY BRUCE ROGERS
FROM
BOOKS AND PAMPHLETS
PRINTED FOR HIM
AT VARIOUS
PRESSES

PLATE 21 Typography for a pamphlet.

PHOTO BY ISRAEL SCHENKER. COURTESY OF THE MELBERT B. CARY, JR. GRAPHIC ARTS COLLECTION, RIT

JOSEPH BLUMENTHAL

Joseph Blumenthal founded The Spiral Press with a partner, George Hoffman, in 1926. He was 28 years old (born 4 October 1897). Two years earlier, he had decided that the traditional business world, in which he was making significant strides, was not for him. His mother had instilled in him a love of books and literature, and it was in the world of books that he went to look for a more rewarding livelihood. After about two years of apprenticing at assorted printing and publishing establishments (including Huebsch, the publisher of James Joyce's early work in the United States), Blumenthal felt that the time had come to strike out on his own. The experience gained during those years before the opening of The Spiral Press proved invaluable, particularly the time spent at the venerable Printing House of William Edwin Rudge in Mount Vernon, New York. Rudge's was arguably the finest press in the country at the time. In the 1920s Bruce Rogers worked there. Blumenthal was fond of telling the story of how he worked directly under Rogers at Rudge: Rogers's office was on the second floor while Blumenthal toiled in the composing room on the first floor!

A brief stint at The Marchbanks Press in New York City followed. Blumenthal gained not only useful printing experience, but also a partner. George Hoffman was plant superintendent at Marchbanks. At first he was not pleased to meet Blumenthal, since the proprietor had neglected to inform him of the new hire, but soon Hoffman and Blumenthal discovered they had many common interests and aspirations. They agreed to start a small press together. In a few short years, the Great Depression would force Hoffman to secure steady employment with another printer in order to support his family, while Blumenthal went off to Germany to further his studies and produce a private type.

Many would argue that the 1920s was the golden era of American typography. Rudge had a formidable plant producing superlative presswork in combination with the talents of Bruce Rogers, Frederic Warde, Peter Beilenson, and others. There was also The Merrymount Press in Boston under the direction of Daniel Berkeley Updike, John Fass printing at The Harbor Press in New York City, The Press of A. Colish, and the Marchbanks Press, among others. In addition there were free-lance designers such as T. M. Cleland, W. A. Dwiggins, Frederic Goudy, and others. On the West Coast the Grabhorn brothers, John Henry Nash, and Taylor & Taylor were already well established. One would be hard-pressed to find a comparable confluence of fine printing facilities at any other time or place.

It was into this crowded – even saturated – field that Joseph Blumenthal entered. He was ill-equipped to stake his claim in the New York printing world of 1926: a brief apprenticeship at assorted shops offered scant practical knowledge, making his partner George Hoffman's experience invaluable during the formative years of The Spiral Press. Blumenthal's father had left him $5,000, a tidy amount in 1926, which could equip a modest printing office – but it would leave scarce operating capital after outfitting the shop. In addition, Blumenthal did not have the kind of connections that would ensure steady trade for the fledgling press.

Perhaps the key to the survival of The Spiral Press was the fact that they had something which would set them apart from the competition. The dominant style of the era, as we have seen in the work of Updike and Rogers, was firmly rooted in allusive typography. It was William Morris who inspired many of the twentieth-century's printers in this direction. But Morris was a confirmed medievalist, and therefore practiced a dark, heavy style of typography and ornamentation, admittedly to stunning effect. Somewhat later in England, Francis Meynell and Stanley Morison carried allusive typography in other directions. The American typographers Updike and Rogers reached perhaps the greatest height – and breadth – of this style. In their work one can see books inspired by Italian renaissance forms, French baroque, and British and Italian neoclassical typography; even especially crude early American styles were copied and adapted where deemed appropriate. John Fass at the Harbor Press and T. M. Cleland also followed this style – or more accurately styles – perhaps with a somewhat less varied repertoire.

The Spiral Press, however, showed little if any taste for allusive typography. Instead, it endeavored to create a modern, contemporary look, with no archaic elements. While Rogers, Updike, Morison, Meynell, et al. were copying types and decorations from ages past, Blumenthal was importing fresh fonts from Europe, designing a new proprietary face and commissioning contemporary artists to decorate his printing. While the American and British type foundries were feverishly reviving earlier typefaces, Blumenthal was among the first in this country to use new typeface designs such as Koch Antiqua (used at Spiral for the 1927 edition of *Phillida and Coridon*) or Jan van Krimpen's Lutetia type (which was used by Blumenthal in the handsome 1930 edition of the *Complete Poems of Robert Frost*, printed for Random House). This latter book was to be the basis of a friendship between Frost and Blumenthal which lasted until the poet's death in 1963, and which was to be the source of much fine printing done at The Spiral Press, such as *A Sermon* (plate 24), and notably the charming series of Frost / Spiral Christmas booklets (plate 22).

In keeping with a more modern look, Blumenthal used ornaments sparingly, if at all. Often at The Spiral Press a totally unadorned piece would be printed with striking effect. This may be compared to the post-war design aesthetic of Paul Rand or Hermann Zapf, but it was novel in the twenties, thirties, and forties. In this regard Blumenthal stands in great contrast to the other well-known typographers of his era, many of whom could appear to be incapable of designing a piece of printing if it did not have decoration on it. When decoration was used at Spiral, it was most likely to be in the form of a woodcut or linoleum cut by a contemporary artist. Early on, Blumenthal employed several prominent members of the Ashcan School of New York artists, such as Armin Landeck, Emil Ganso, Howard Cook, Reginald Marsh, and Wanda Gág. Later eminent artists such as Ben Shahn (plate 27), Antonio Frasconi, and Leonard Baskin saw some of their first professional work roll off the presses at Spiral. For the occasional piece in which typographic ornament was used at The Spiral Press (which was far less often than in the work of Rogers, Updike, Fass, and others), it tended to be a modern, original design, not a redrawing of some ancient arabesque.

This is not to say that Blumenthal did not have his influences; he most certainly did. There were clear and distinct antecedents to his work. It's just that these precursors were far different from the historical models being imitated by American typographers of the time. Contemporary continental typography was a major influence, and we have already noted that the Press was the first to import from Germany Rudolf Koch's Antiqua type (later to be popularized as "Eve" in the United States). It was used in an assured, contemporary way in The Spiral Press edition of *Phillida and Coridon*, and in many pieces of ephemeral printing. As we have also seen, Spiral was among the first in this country to use Van Krimpen's Lutetia type, as shown in the *Poems of Edgar Allan Poe* (plate 23) and other pieces of its work.

The strongest influence on the early work of The Spiral Press was the printing done by Willy Wiegand at The Bremer Presse in Germany. Blumenthal emulated Wiegand's clean, crisp typography and superlative composition and presswork. Like Wiegand, Blumenthal had his own proprietary type cut by Louis Hoell and cast at the Bauer Typefoundry in Frankfurt, Germany – he even had the initial trial settings printed at The Bremer Presse. A relatively deeply toned, laid handmade paper, similar to that used by The Bremer Presse, was manufactured by the same mill (Zanders) and imported into this country for Spiral Press books. However, Blumenthal's printing did have its significant differences when compared to The Bremer Presse model: Spiral's work was in many respects more universal and less precious as compared to the aristocratic work of The Bremer Presse. The Spiral type (later re-cut for the Monotype composing machine and called Emerson) it is less mannered and more restful than the Bremer font; see plates 24, 27 & 30), is certainly more typographic / inscriptional, and less calligraphic. Emerson can still be seen used to good effect today, while the Bremer font – like almost all private press typefaces – is nearly forgotten.

In one of those ironic instances where adversity offers an unexpected opportunity, it was the Great Depression that gave Blumenthal the chance to create his own type. Despite the fact that fine printing is, essentially, a luxury item, The Spiral Press was able to survive the early years of the Depression relatively well. By January of 1931, however, the harsh economic realities hit the business, and the shop was closed down. As mentioned before, George Hoffman found gainful employment elsewhere. Blumenthal put the Press's equipment in storage and travelled with his wife, Ann, to Europe, where he visited many of the great printers of the day and worked on his typeface design.

On his way back to America, Blumenthal stopped over in England, where he met several of the great British typographers, including Stanley Morison who was then typographical advisor to the British Monotype Corporation. Morison thought well enough of Blumenthal's new type to have it cut in several sizes for machine casting on the Monotype. He did this despite the fact that he realized modern types in general did not sell nearly as well as historical revivals, but he felt it his mission to include some contemporary types, such as Gill's Perpetua and Van Krimpen's Lutetia, in Monotype's type development program. Morison's assessment was to prove accurate: Emerson sold only forty sets of matrices, making it a loss leader for Monotype.

While the influence of Koch, Wiegand, and Van Krimpen was evident in the work of The Spiral Press in the early years, Blumenthal did not stop growing beyond these styles. Eventually a new influence emerged and developed into a unique, recognizable look that would become associated with the Press, but this was actually one of several "looks." The clear, rational fonts and typography of eighteenth-century England were employed at the Press for a new, strong, American style, combining well-leaded Baskerville text type with meticulously letterspaced Bulmer capitals – along with the occasional swelled rule. This was to become one hallmark of Spiral Press typography. Despite the fact that this combination is so readily recognizable as a classic Spiral Press style, only nine of the sixty-five books exhibited in the 1966 Morgan Library exhibition, *The Spiral Press Through Four Decades*, use it (see plate 32, showing these elements used for the catalogue's design). Blumenthal's own typeface design (Emerson or Spiral), which is of a far different renaissance pedigree, is more prevalent, being used in twenty percent (or thirteen) of the titles exhibited (as in *The Alphabet of Creation*, plate 27). Even the ubiquitous Garamond is used almost as much as Baskerville and Bulmer, making an appearance in seven instances. So it is really unfair to assign a standard typographic look to The Spiral Press's printing. Actually, a wide variety of styles are evident, from classic private press layouts, employing strong, simple types on beautiful handmade papers; to neoclassical Baskerville and Bulmer styles; to fresh and modern asymmetric layouts (for example, *Grolier 75*, plate 31), occasionally employing a sans-serif font.

After Blumenthal reopened his press in the 1940s new continental typography continued to inspire his work. He was among the first to lay in his cases such important German types as Weiss roman and Hermann Zapf's Palatino italic, Sistina (*Chinese Calligraphy and Painting*, plate 28), and Michelangelo Titling. All were used in novel and attractive ways. Modern, fresh typographic design consistently poured forth from The Spiral Press until Blumenthal closed the doors for good in 1971, when he was seventy-four years old and had reached the heights of printing in America during nearly five decades of productive work. He then turned his attention to writing several books on the history of printing – some of which have become classics in the field – and to an occasional book design.

The close relationship between The Spiral Press and many of the finest American artists of its day is unique in the annals of printing in the United States. In Germany The Cranach Presse had close ties with sculptor and woodcut artist Aristide Maillol, and the English wood engraver, Eric Gill. In England, The Golden Cockerel Press worked with Gill and many other fine wood engravers; The Nonesuch Press employed the talents of Edward McKnight Kauffer, Paul Nash, George Grosz, Reynolds Stone, and others; and in France books illustrated by artists of the stature of Picasso, Matisse, Léger, Rouault, and scores more set the standard for artists' books; but in America, there was little activity of this kind until fairly recently.

The Spiral Press, however, became a haven in this country for artists interested in the book. The first book printed at the Press, *Primitives*, was a combination of woodcuts and poems by the German / American cubist artist, Max Weber. It is generally considered the first American *livre d'artiste*, earning the distinction of being the initial item in The Grolier Club's comprehensive 1993 exhibition of *The American Livre de Peintre*. Previously we mentioned the artists of the Ashcan School who worked with The Spiral Press in the early years. Later famous artists such as Ben Shahn and Alexander Calder (plate 26) were also to develop close relationships with the Press and its proprietor.

Spiral became a catalyst in the development of two eminent artists who began their careers in the fifties: both Leonard Baskin and Antonio Frasconi were virtually unknown when they began their association with Blumenthal, and both would later gladly acknowledge their debt to him. After Blumenthal's death on 4 July 1990, Baskin wrote: "My deepest and most enduring memory of Joe is of his great kindness and easy goodness and of his commendable patience with an unknowing, if wildly ambitious neophyte."

Joseph Blumenthal founded The Spiral Press at a time when the standards were high and the competition was keen – perhaps keener than ever. He unassumingly pursued a different, more modern and freer style than his contemporaries. German typographer Gustav Stresow wrote in a 1979 article published in *Philobiblon* that "Blumenthal was the best printer of his generation in America." That's quite a statement, and one that can be borne out by a review of his work over a productive half-century.

*

As we have seen, on his stopover in England in 1931 Blumenthal showed Stanley Morison proofs of his Spiral type, and Morison proposed to have Monotype cut the design for machine composition. This would result in the Emerson font. Aside from his expertise in type design and its history, Morison was himself an influential book designer. Through his work at various English publishers such as Burns & Oates, Ernest Benn, and most significantly the Cambridge University Press, he promoted a clear, workman-like style, paying attention to materials and typographic nuances all too often overlooked in book design.

A YOUNG BIRCH

ROBERT FROST

PLATE 22   One of the Spiral Press / Robert Frost Christmas booklets.

Poems of Edgar Allan Poe

With an introduction by Howard Mumford Jones

༈ 1929 ༈

The Spiral Press · New York

PLATE 23   An early Spiral Press book, 1929, set in the then-new Lutetia font, designed by Jan van Krimpen.

44

A SERMON BY Robert Frost

SPOKEN ON THE FIRST DAY OF

THE FEAST OF TABERNACLES AT

THE ROCKDALE AVENUE TEMPLE

CINCINNATI · OHIO · THURSDAY

MORNING · OCTOBER · 10 · 1946

PLATE 24 Joseph Blumenthal's Emerson typeface in a modern, asymmetric design.

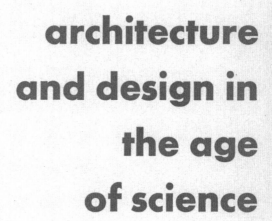

architecture
and design in
the age
of science

BY WALTER GROPIUS

PLATE 25 Contemporary treatment of a modern subject.

A BESTIARY

COMPILED BY RICHARD WILBUR

ILLUSTRATED BY ALEXANDER CALDER

PRINTED AT THE SPIRAL PRESS FOR Pantheon Books
NEW YORK

PLATE 26 A modern title page in the Bulmer typeface.

THE ALPHABET
OF CREATION

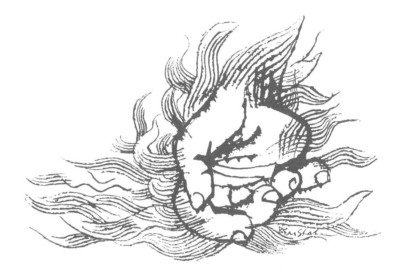

An ancient legend from the Zohar

with drawings by BEN SHAHN.

Printed at The Spiral Press and

published by Pantheon, New York.

PLATE 27   A typical example of the collaboration between artist (Ben Shahn) and printer (Joseph Blumenthal).

CHINESE

CALLIGRAPHY AND

PAINTING

IN THE COLLECTION OF

JOHN M. CRAWFORD, JR.

NEW YORK · 1962

PLATE 28 Title page set in Hermann Zapf's Sistina Titling typeface.

A BOY'S WILL
BY ROBERT FROST

HENRY HOLT AND COMPANY
NEW YORK

PLATE 29 One of the earlier Blumenthal / Robert Frost collaborations.

PHYSIOLOGUS THEOBALDI EPISCOPI

DE NATURIS DUODECIM ANIMALIUM

THE LATIN TEXT · AN ENGLISH TRANSLATION

BY WILLIS BARNSTONE · WITH WOODCUTS AND

LITHOGRAPHS BY RUDY POZZATTI

PUBLISHED BY INDIANA UNIVERSITY PRESS

BLOOMINGTON

PLATE 30 Set in Blumenthal's Emerson typeface.

GROLIER

A BIOGRAPHICAL RETRO-SPECTIVE TO CELEBRATE THE SEVENTY-FIFTH ANNI-VERSARY OF THE GROLIER CLUB IN NEW YORK

PLATE 31 Perpetua Titling type with hand-lettered "75" by Philip Grushkin.

THE
SPIRAL
PRESS

THROUGH FOUR DECADES

AN EXHIBITION OF BOOKS AND

EPHEMERA · WITH A COMMENTARY

BY JOSEPH BLUMENTHAL

THE PIERPONT MORGAN LIBRARY

NEW YORK 1966

PLATE 32 Title page in Bulmer type with a swelled rule – a Blumenthal favorite.

Eight of the eleven twentieth-century book designers discussed in this book also designed important typefaces. (Rogers designed Centaur among a few other fonts; Blumenthal, Emerson; Morison, Times New Roman; Mardersteig, Dante; Van Krimpen, Lutetia, Spectrum, Romulus, and others; Tschichold, Sabon; and Zapf, Palatino, Optima, Renaissance, and many others). The remaining four book designers had close connections with type manufacturers, or even with the development of specific typefaces: Updike commissioned two private types for his Merrymount Press; Meynell initiated the production of Plantin Light with long ascenders and descenders, as well as Fournier with smaller capitals (first used in his Nonesuch Press edition of the complete works of Shakespeare); Caflisch designed the open titling font Columna, and was closely associated with the type division at Hell GmbH (in addition, his handwriting was adapted by Robert Slimbach at Adobe Systems into a typeface called "Caflisch Script"); and many of the Stempel Foundry's post-war types were first used in books and other printed material designed by Gotthard de Beauclair. Of our subjects, three – Van Krimpen, Zapf, and Morison – are best known for their work in typeface design, yet each made significant contributions to the design of printed books in the twentieth century.

Like his close friend Daniel Berkeley Updike, Stanley Morison came to printing with few, if any, advantages. He was born on 6 May 1889 into a poor family, and the family's circumstances necessitated his leaving school in 1903, at the age of fourteen. It is quite an achievement that the man who would become one of the greatest scholars of printing of his time – in addition to becoming an expert on book typography and type design, as well as member of the editorial board of the London *Times*, had so little formal education.

In September of 1912 Morison came across a special supplement on printing published by *The Times*, and that would change his life. Much in the same way that seeing Kelmscott Press books crystallized Bruce Rogers's focus for the rest of his life, so this defining moment was the catalyst for a lifetime involvement for Morison. A few months after seeing the 1912 special printing supplement, he would answer an advertisement for an assistant at the offices of the printing journal *The Imprint*. This would turn out to be the beginning of a career in fine printing and type design which would last more than half a century and influence the course of those crafts thereafter.

Interestingly, the advertisement specified "the services of a young man of good education and preferably of some experience in publishing and advertising," qualifications which Morison did not possess. Instead, when he was asked by Gerard Meynell (a cousin of Francis Meynell's, whom we will discuss in the next chapter) of *The Imprint* why he wanted the job, he replied that he was tired of being a bank clerk. Meynell, having been a bank clerk himself, sympathized and gave Morison the job – his first big break in the field of typography.

The Imprint, while influential, was short-lived. Morison's first article – the first of hundreds – "Notes on Some Liturgical Books," appeared in August 1913 in the eighth (and penultimate) number. Before *The Imprint* closed Meynell arranged for Morison to begin work as a typographer at the offices of the religious publishers Burns & Oates, where his uncle Wilfrid was a partner. There Morison was able to develop his skills as a book designer. At Burns & Oates he also became close friends with Wilfrid's son, Francis. They had many common interests and tastes in typography, favoring the historical study of types and printing as a basis for contemporary design. Both men would go on to become renowned book designers in their own rights (albeit via very different paths – Meynell making his name mainly as publisher of fine editions, Morison working for several quality trade and university publishers, in addition to supervising typeface development for a major corporation). They collaborated on several pieces of printing at Burns & Oates and later at The Pelican Press, where Francis was in charge of design. In addition, they coauthored an article on "Printers' Flowers and Arabesques" for the first issue of *The Fleuron,* the great journal of typography of the 1920s (the last three numbers of the annual were edited and designed by Morison). This interest in historical styles and printers' arabesque ornaments can be seen in quite a few of Morison's earlier book designs (see plate 42).

In 1916, Francis Meynell founded The Pelican Press, to which he brought his friend Stanley Morison. In 1919 Meynell temporarily vacated his position at Pelican, leaving Morison in charge of design. Then, when Meynell returned in 1920, Morison moved on to the newly formed Cloister Press, where he would produce attractive promotional material (much of it with text on the typefaces displayed written in a clear, informative style by Morison himself). The Cloister Press was also where he would form an important association with the plant's manager, Walter Lewis. Lewis was later to become manager of the printing works at the Cambridge University Press, where Morison was to collaborate with him on much fine printing.

A key aspect of Morison's typography was his embrace of machine methods – including machine typesetting – even for the highest standard of fine printing. The same can be said of Meynell and others, but, amazing as it may now seem, in the early part of the century there were many who believed that only handset type was suitable for the highest grade work, and that machine composition was antithetical to the Kelmscott-Doves-Ashendene devotion to hand craftsmanship. Keep in mind that Updike did not use a Monotype font until 1925 (by which time his Merrymount Press had been in existence for more than thirty years), and Rogers not until 1919 – but both Monotype and Linotype composition had been readily available since the 1890s. Bernard Newdigate of the Shakespeare Head Press left the then-forming Fleuron Publishing Society when Morison and Meynell (among others) would not agree with his contention that handset type was superior to machine composition. Morison's openness to machine composition would prove instrumental to his career and the development of typography in the twentieth century, as we shall see.

In 1922, Morison was retained by the British Monotype Corporation as typographical advisor. There he was to institute a program of typeface production including revivals of historic types which he found worthy of manufacture, together with new designs by Van Krimpen, Gill, Blumenthal, and others that would become key typographic materials throughout the century and beyond. By producing typefaces such as Poliphilus, Bembo, Bell, Gill Sans, Fournier, Baskerville (see plate 34), and his own Times New Roman design, among others, Morison's work at Monotype would influence the course of fine printing from that time on. Sebastian Carter has concisely summarized Morison's achievement in the field of type design:

It would be impossible to write about type design in [the twentieth] century without mentioning him, and even though he himself designed only one typeface, and that in a somewhat once removed manner, that typeface was Times New Roman which, although figures are impossible to come by and compare, is arguably the most widely-used roman typeface in the world.

The next year, in 1923, Morison was hired by the Cambridge University Press as its typographical advisor (a position which was established upon the recommendation of Bruce Rogers in his report on Cambridge typography made in 1917). At Cambridge he would do much of his finest book design, including several seminal books for which he was author of the text as well as designer. His monograph on John Bell (plate 36) – the eighteenth-century publisher who was also responsible for the typeface which today bears his name – is a good example of Morison's myriad talents. He designed the book and wrote the text containing important new information on a key figure in the history of printing, typography and newspapers, using the Stephenson Blake version of Bell which he had identified. The Monotype version, which Morison initiated, followed the next year. The book was beautifully printed on handmade paper at the Cambridge University Press, with illustrations reproduced by a variety of processes including intaglio, collotype, and hand coloring – some even printed on a different paper to more accurately match the original and then tipped in.

Morison's tenets of book design were simple and concise: first was the choice of a legible type, without eccentricities, next, an attention to the often-overlooked details of good printing, such as proper imposition and careful presswork, and finally an attractive arrangement of all elements with harmonious materials and binding. Anything at all flashy was certainly not to his taste in book design. His work is often somewhat quiet (see plate 41), and that's how he liked it. You will never see splashy colors, extremely large or unusual types, or attention-getting gimmicks in Morison's book typography. However, some of his advertising typography, including his famous dust jackets for the publisher Victor Gollancz (plate 39), are quite a different story – there Morison would let go with a riot of bright color, and all kinds of unusual types mixed in unusual ways. Still, book typography was a different thing for him (as it should be). When he did have the opportunity to incorporate more bravura into a fine book production, he most often opted for fine papers and attractive inserts printed on assorted stocks in various colors and types (as in *John Bell*, 1930; the last three issues of *The Fleuron*, which he edited from 1927 to 1930; and his monumental five-volume deluxe issue of the *History of the Times*, 1935–52). Being an expert on letterforms, both typographic and calligraphic, Morison would occasionally incorporate some hand-lettering on the title page, headings, or colophon of a book he designed in order to relieve the generally quiet consistency of pure typography. However, he saw a keen distinction between written and cut lettering, and therefore often employed a letter cutter such as Reynolds Stone (1909–1979) to engrave lettering for a title page (plate 40).

Morison's beliefs were spelled out clearly and succinctly in his brief essay "First Principles of Typography," originally published in *The Fleuron* No. 7 (1930). It is interesting to note that this surprisingly popular short manifesto (it has been reprinted dozens of times and translated into eight languages) deals mainly with book typography, yet the title refers to typography in general – not a specific branch of the typographic arts. "First Principles" contains several nuggets of timeless wisdom: "Typography is an efficient means to an essentially utilitarian and only accidentally aesthetic end"; "Imposition is the most important element in typography"; "The history of printing is in large measure the history of the title-page"; "To an inventive printer decoration is not often necessary"; etc.) as well as some dicta which are perhaps statements of Morison's humility and personal style rather than universally adhered-to tenets ("Any disposition of printing material which, whatever the intention, has the effect of coming between author and reader is wrong"; "In [the printer's] humble job, individualism is not very helpful"; "There is no reason . . . for a title-page to bear any line of type larger than twice the size of the text letter"; etc.).

Morison's is a recognizably British style. His best books have to be seen to be adequately appreciated, for only by handling the materials and seeing the superior workmanship firsthand can one begin to appreciate his productions. Of course the same can be said for all fine book work, where paper, type, presswork, and binding combine to create a visual and tactile entity that cannot be fully reproduced, yet somehow this is even truer in Morison's case, where all the elements are subtly orchestrated to form an attractive whole. His work in this manner was a great influence on British book production of the twentieth century. And it would be hard to overrate the influence of the typefaces which he initiated and saw through production. Even today many of the best typefaces available – fonts such as Bembo, Fournier, Times New Roman, Eric Gill's Perpetua, and the British Monotype versions of Baskerville and Garamond – fonts which all told may account for a majority of those used in fine bookwork – come from the programme Morison initiated at Monotype three-quarters of a century ago. He died on 12 October 1967, one day after his monumental study of the Fell types was published.

*

Stanley Morison's career in printing began humbly enough when he answered an ad for an assistant at *The Imprint*, the journal of printing founded by Gerard Meynell, among others, in January of 1913. The journal lasted a mere nine issues, but it had an impact far beyond its brief lifespan. As previously mentioned, Meynell hired Morison for the job, despite the fact that he had virtually none of the experience requested for the position. Before the journal ceased publication, Meynell found Morison another job, at the publishing firm of Burns & Oates, which was run by his uncle, Wilfrid Meynell. Wilfrid had put his son Francis in charge of book production; he and Morison soon realized that they had many interests in common, and they became close associates – though both would soon go their separate ways: Morison to make typographic history at the British Monotype Corporation and the Cambridge University Press, and his younger friend (Francis Meynell was two years his junior) to The Pelican Press. Shortly thereafter Francis Meynell established his famous publishing house, The Nonesuch Press, where he would prove that modern machine-based methods could be used in the production of fine printing – something that had previously been reserved for handicraft methods only.

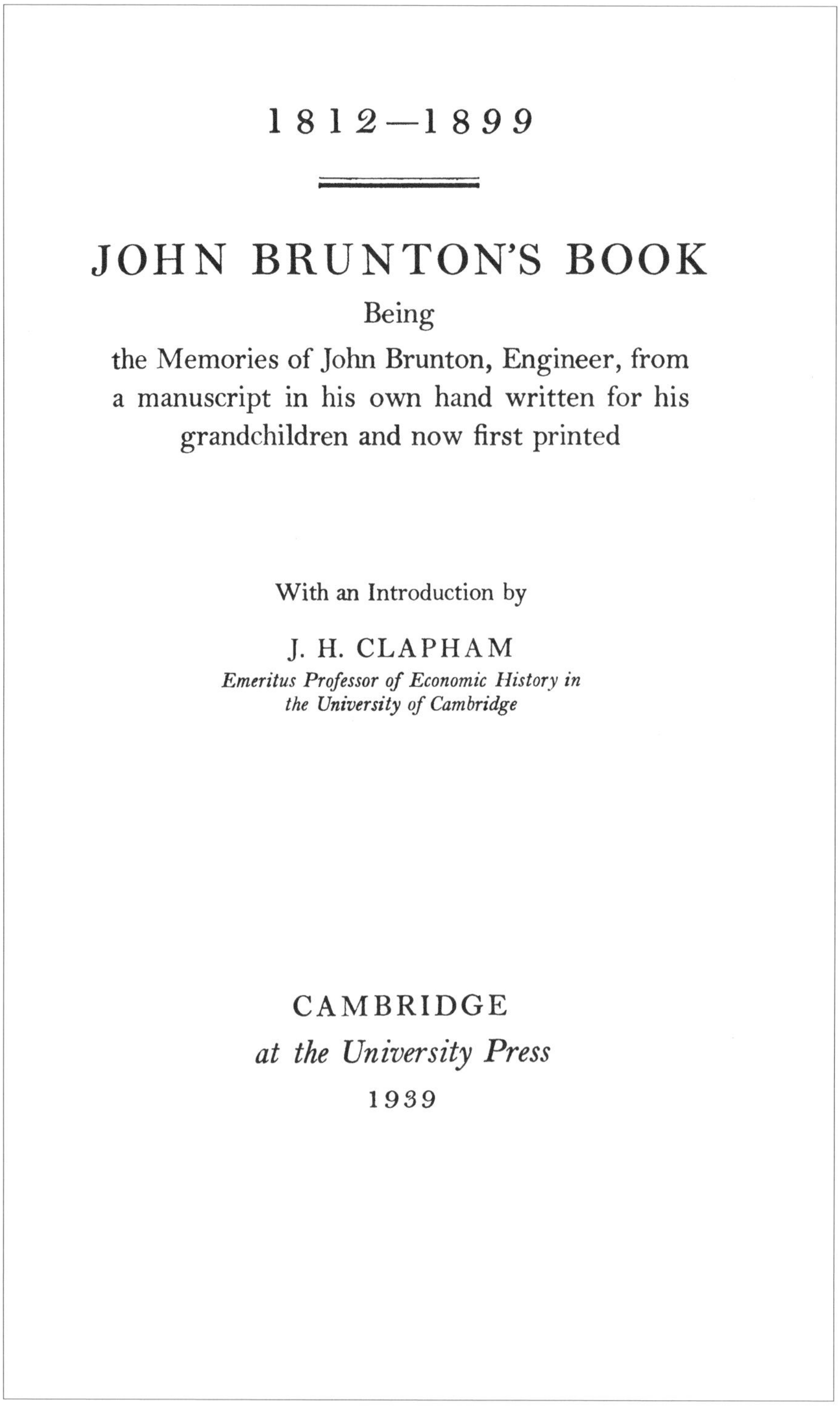

1812—1899

JOHN BRUNTON'S BOOK

Being

the Memories of John Brunton, Engineer, from
a manuscript in his own hand written for his
grandchildren and now first printed

With an Introduction by

J. H. CLAPHAM

*Emeritus Professor of Economic History in
the University of Cambridge*

CAMBRIDGE
at the University Press
1939

PLATE 33 A representative Morison title page for the Cambridge University Press.

A SPECIMEN

OF

PRINTING LETTER

DESIGNED BY

John Baskerville

ABOUT THE YEAR MDCCLVII

RECUT BY

THE LANSTON

MONOTYPE CORPORATION

LIMITED FOR USE ON THE

"MONOTYPE"

LONDON

43 AND 44 FETTER LANE E.C.4

MCMXXVI

PLATE 34 Specimen of one of the typefaces Morison was responsible for reviving at the British Monotype Corporation.

BREVIARIUM ROMANUM

EX DECRETO SS. CONCILII TRIDENTINI
RESTITUTUM S. PII V PONT. MAX. JUSSU
EDITUM ALIORUM PONTIFICUM CURA
RECOGNITUM DENIQUE PII PAPÆ X
AUCTORITATE REFORMATUM

EDITIONIS
JUXTA TYPICAM CONFECTÆ
PARS VERNA

LONDINI
APUD BURNS OATES & WASHBOURNE
EDITORES LIBRORUM PONTIFICIOS
MCMXLVI

PLATE 35 Wood-engraved title and crest by Reynolds Stone.

JOHN  BELL

BOOKSELLER & PART-PROPRIETOR IN
THE MORNING POST, ETC.

The career of John Bell as a bookseller seems to have opened before he was twenty-four years of age, and as a newspaper-proprietor before he was twenty-seven. The earliest indication of his activities which I have been able to find is his receipt "for Four Pounds in full for one half of my 16th share of Francis's Horace bought at Millar's Sale." The receipt is dated Sept. 13, 1769. An early imprint, "Printed for John Bell in the Strand," figures in Kenrick's *Free Thoughts on Seduction*. In 1772 he published *The Universal Catalogue*, "printed for the proprietors and sold by J. Bell near Exeter 'Change in the Strand," an octavo chronicle of current literature compiled from the *Critical Review* and the *Monthly Review*. Lengthy notices from these are appended to the title, author's name, date and place of publication. The compilation is important in the history of Catalogues and valuable as an Index to Current Literature. It is characteristic of Bell that he

1   1

PLATE 36   The first text page for Morison's seminal work on John Bell.

THE
ELIZABETHAN
ZOO

A
BOOK OF BEASTS
BOTH
FABULOUS
AND
AUTHENTIC

LONDON
FREDERICK ETCHELLS & HUGH MACDONALD
1A KENSINGTON PLACE · W.8
1926

PLATE 37   Ingenious border composed of lowercase Blado italic z's.

KENSINGTON
GARDENS

by

HUMBERT WOLFE

ERNEST BENN LTD.

8 Bouverie Street, E.C.

1924

PLATE 38 Another novel border treatment.

THE
intelligentsia
OF GREAT BRITAIN
BY DMITRI MIRSKY
(ci-devant Prince Mirsky)

including estimates of

Bernard Shaw	Eddington
H. G. Wells	**Jeans**
J. M. Keynes	Cole
G. K. Chesterton	E. M. FORSTER
Bertrand Russell	*Lytton Strachey*
D. H. LAWRENCE	T. S. Eliot
Aldous Huxley	Dean Inge
Virginia Woolf	Laski
WYNDHAM LEWIS	**MALINOWSKY**
Middleton Murry	

&c. &c.

W e (the publishers) ask our friends to forgive us:
we don't agree with **everything**

~~Prince~~ MIRSKY says.

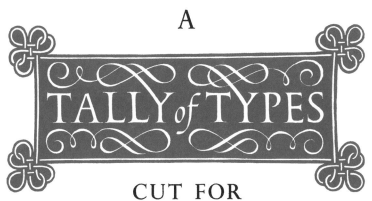

A

TALLY of TYPES

CUT FOR
MACHINE COMPOSITION
AND
INTRODUCED AT
THE UNIVERSITY PRESS
CAMBRIDGE

1922-1932

CAMBRIDGE
PRIVATELY PRINTED
1953

PLATE 40 One of the Cambridge University Press Christmas books, with lettering engraved on wood by Reynolds Stone in combination with Perpetua capitals.

SAMUEL TAYLOR COLERIDGE

THE RIME OF THE ANCIENT MARINER

with ten engravings on copper

by

DAVID JONES

BRISTOL

DOUGLAS CLEVERDON

1929

PLATE 41   A sparse title page, set in Frederic Warde's Arrighi type.

EARLY
SPANISH BALLADS IN THE BRITISH MUSEUM

III

Romance
de don Gayferos

printed by J. CROMBERGER *Seville c.* 1515

With introduction, and variant readings
from another Seville edition
and a Valencia edition
of *c.* 1540
Edited
by
HENRY THOMAS

MCMXXVII

PLATE 42   An ornate treatment (two years earlier than the illustration on the facing page).

Francis Meynell was born on 12 May 1891 into a literary family. His mother, Alice, was a poet, quite well respected in her day, though few are now aware of her writing. His father, Wilfrid, was a journalist, and also a principal at the Catholic publishers Burns & Oates – a position which would prove of immense importance to the young Francis. Wilfrid's nephew, Gerard, was a man of great stature in the fine printing field, being associated with the Westminster Press, co-editor of a seminal journal on printing called *The Imprint*, in addition to being involved in the production of two significant typefaces: Imprint (an adaptation of Caslon originally created for the composition of *The Imprint*), and Johnston Underground Sans (designed mainly by the great calligrapher Edward Johnston and still in use today by the London Underground). These roots would grow into an important career in book design.

Francis's initiation into book production came in 1912, when his father employed him at Burns & Oates. There he began with minor errands, but soon he was involved in the layout of some well-designed books. Of particular note from this era is *Ordo Administrandi Sacramenta* with the large titling lines on the title page cut in wood by Eric Gill. In 1916, Meynell founded The Pelican Press, where a true indication of his mature typographic style would manifest itself in several publications, such as *Typography* (1923, plate 43; mainly written by Meynell himself), *The Pervigilium Veneris* (1924), and the extremely handsome Pelican Press type specimen broadside. The use of printer's piece ornaments, with historical types and decoration derived mainly from sixteenth- and seventeenth-century sources (such as in plates 49 and 50), were the hallmarks of a style that would become evident in many of Meynell's book designs. Allusive typography, so ably practiced by Updike and Rogers, was also prominent in the work of Francis Meynell. As he said, "Bruce Rogers, the great American typographer, was my hero." At The Pelican Press Meynell was applying Rogers's principles to books printed in England, as well as all manner of commercial printing.

While Meynell found satisfaction in book design and typography through his work at Burns & Oates and Pelican (as well as his small private press, the Romney Street Press), he longed to make fine editions of literature available – and affordable – for a wider public. He wrote to several publishers suggesting that they sponsor a division where he could produce these fine editions of English classics, an offer which none took up. So he decided that if no publisher would start such an imprint, he would do it himself. With the help of a partner, David Garnett, and capital supplied by his first wife, Vera, Meynell launched what was to become the most important publishing program of his life, and one that would be a model – both editorially and aesthetically – for many others to follow.

In 1923 Meynell published an edition of the *Love Poems of John Donne,* the first volume in a series of more than 100 titles to be issued by The Nonesuch Press. From the beginning The Nonesuch Press was different from any of its predecessors. First, it wasn't truly a press, in the way that Kelmscott, Doves, Merrymount, and even Riverside were – it had no significant holdings of type or presses. It is true that it had a small amount of Janson type on the premises, and that once or twice the Press even set a short book with its own type, but almost all the production of The Nonesuch Press was done by outside contractors. Second, its editions were far lengthier than previous private press editions, usually hovering around eight or nine hundred copies, and sometimes up to 1,500 or more. One Nonesuch title, *The Week-End Book,* eventually sold an astonishing 100,000 copies! In these ways, Nonesuch was more of a publisher than a private press. There was, however, one key similarity between Nonesuch and other private presses: one person (in this case Francis Meynell) oversaw and controlled all aspects of the design and production of every Nonesuch title – until the sale of the company to George Macy in 1936. During his years at Nonesuch, Meynell was to set a style not too far removed from the books he had designed previously for Pelican and Burns & Oates.

A major difference was that at Nonesuch, with its large quantity of titles, Meynell had the opportunity to expand his range considerably. Some titles (such as *The Book of Ruth,* 1923; *Kisses,* 1923; or *In Memoriam* by Tennyson, 1933, plate 49) are indistinguishable in style from his earlier work; others show perhaps a more developed design style (such as *Mother Goose,* 1925; Rousseau, 1938, plate 48; or *The Greek Portrait,* 1934, plate 47); and still others display an attempt to be truly modern, something in which Meynell was perhaps not entirely successful (see, for example, *The Devil and All,* 1934 plate 45; or *Benito Cereno,* 1926). Meynell's edition of *Genesis* (plate 44), with Paul Nash's woodcuts working in harmony with Rudolf Koch's rugged Neuland typeface, is possibly the most successful of his more modern book designs.

By publishing fine editions in larger quantities than had been previously attempted, Meynell was able to amortize the costs of quality production over a long run, giving him great cost savings which he passed on to Nonesuch customers. He also employed newer machine composition and printing technologies to his advantage, thereby being able to offer books at a lower price while losing little or nothing in the way of quality. Dividing his work up amongst many of the best printers also afforded

Meynell an exceptionally wide range of typefaces, materials, and processes to choose from. This gave Nonesuch books a variety which was unprecedented at the time. Meynell also promoted the Nonesuch editions more professionally than most of the fine edition publishers who preceeded him, issuing handsome prospectuses at least once a year, and advertising in various periodicals.

The textual content of the works of various book designers is beyond the scope of this book, but special mention should be made of the high editorial standards at Nonesuch. Meynell championed several great British writers, such as Donne and Blake, and produced a scrupulously edited complete Shakespeare, as well as publishing new works by a variety of authors. Significant editions of previously unpublished texts (such as the *153 Letters from W. H. Hudson* or D. H. Lawrence's *Love Among the Haystacks*) were published alongside literary anthologies containing previously printed material (such as the *Latin Portrait* and the *Greek Portrait*, plate 47). The Nonesuch Compendium series made available the texts of a dozen writers, each in one handy, well-made volume selling for a modest price.

For some time the Nonesuch formula proved quite successful – a good harbinger for other fine bookmakers. But the Depression inevitably took its toll on an essentially luxury item like the finely printed book, so in 1936 Meynell sold the Nonesuch imprint to American George Macy, who in 1929 had founded The Limited Editions Club based partially on Meynell's Nonesuch model. Over the next few years, several titles were published under the Nonesuch imprint, with varying degrees of Meynell's involvement, but without the cohesive oversight of the one guiding figure. In 1950, Macy generously restored the Nonesuch imprint to Meynell, and a very different Nonesuch Press published some interesting books in the 1950s and 1960s, many of which were again relatively affordable editions of well-made books – a continuing theme in Meynell's work (see the more modest, but nevertheless exceptionally well-designed editions of the Bible, 1963, and Shakespeare, 1953, compared with their earlier Nonesuch counterparts of 1925–27 and 1929–33 respectively). Several of the later titles, however, such as the collection of Francis Meynell's own poetry entitled *Poems & Pieces* (1961) or the second series of Blake's drawings (1956) could easily be mistaken for pre-war Nonesuch editions. Meynell died in 1975.

Meynell was one of the more flamboyant personalities to inhabit the field of book design – a discipline which generally attracts sterner sorts. His autobiography, *My Lives*, gives a broad picture of his career and character. It is fortunate that Francis Meynell did devote a good part of his youth to an extraordinary publishing venture, where top-notch book design resulted in a substantial series of fine editions.

*

73

The early connection between Meynell and Morison was crucial to the development of both men. Their co-written article "Printers' Flowers and Arabesques," which appeared in the first number of *The Fleuron*, was a testimony to their common interests in decorative materials used by printers. It is impressive how key Morison's influence was to many in the field, including Meynell and Blumenthal, as we have seen, to say nothing of Updike, who was one of Morison's closest friends in the typographic world.

Another close friend of Morison's was Hans (later Giovanni) Mardersteig, whom Morison first visited at Montagnola, in Switzerland, at Christmas, 1924. It was the beginning of a friendship that would last a lifetime. Mardersteig would dedicate his 1969 reprinting of Pietro Bembo's tract *De Aetna* – known for its use of the seminal Aldine/Griffo roman font in the 1495 first printing – to the memory of Morison. Surely no one put Morison's typographic dictums of classic yet original typography, soundly based on the traditions of the past, into finer practice than Mardersteig, first at his private press, The Officina Bodoni, and also later at the Stamperia Valdonega, its sister machine-printing operation.

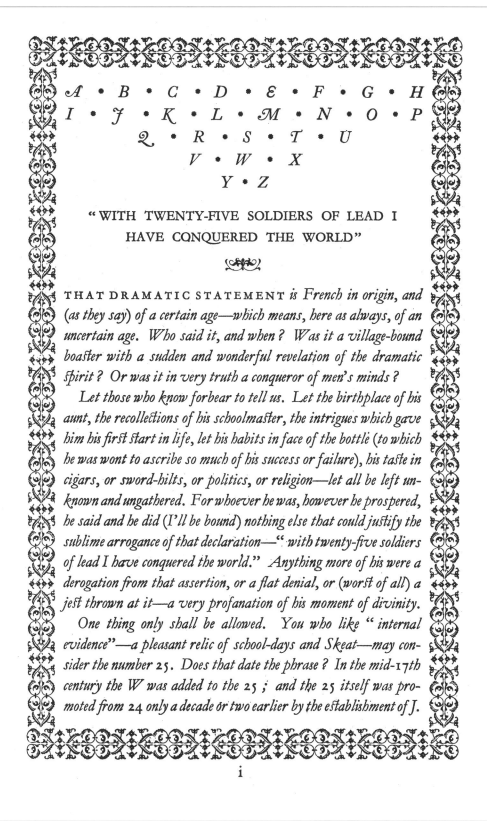

A • B • C • D • E • F • G • H
I • J • K • L • M • N • O • P
Q • R • S • T • U
V • W • X
Y • Z

"WITH TWENTY-FIVE SOLDIERS OF LEAD I
HAVE CONQUERED THE WORLD"

THAT DRAMATIC STATEMENT *is French in origin, and
(as they say) of a certain age—which means, here as always, of an
uncertain age. Who said it, and when? Was it a village-bound
boaster with a sudden and wonderful revelation of the dramatic
spirit? Or was it in very truth a conqueror of men's minds?*

*Let those who know forbear to tell us. Let the birthplace of his
aunt, the recollections of his schoolmaster, the intrigues which gave
him his first start in life, let his habits in face of the bottle (to which
he was wont to ascribe so much of his success or failure), his taste in
cigars, or sword-hilts, or politics, or religion—let all be left unknown and ungathered. For whoever he was, however he prospered,
he said and he did (I'll be bound) nothing else that could justify the
sublime arrogance of that declaration—" with twenty-five soldiers
of lead I have conquered the world." Anything more of his were a
derogation from that assertion, or a flat denial, or (worst of all) a
jest thrown at it—a very profanation of his moment of divinity.*

*One thing only shall be allowed. You who like " internal
evidence"—a pleasant relic of school-days and Skeat—may consider the number 25. Does that date the phrase? In the mid-17th
century the W was added to the 25; and the 25 itself was promoted from 24 only a decade or two earlier by the establishment of J.*

i

PLATE 43 *Typography.* London: The Pelican Press, 1923. Text and layout by Francis Meynell.

AND GOD SAID LET THERE BE
LIGHTS IN THE FIRMAMENT OF THE
HEAVEN TO DIVIDE THE DAY
FROM THE NIGHT AND LET THEM
BE FOR SIGNS AND FOR SEASONS
AND FOR DAYS AND YEARS » AND
LET THEM BE FOR LIGHTS IN THE
FIRMAMENT OF THE HEAVEN TO
GIVE LIGHT UPON THE EARTH AND
IT WAS SO » AND GOD MADE TWO
GREAT LIGHTS THE GREATER LIGHT
TO RULE THE DAY AND THE LESSER
LIGHT TO RULE THE NIGHT
HE MADE THE
STARS ALSO

PLATE 44   *Genesis.* London: The Nonesuch Press, 1924. Woodcuts by Paul Nash on facing pages.

THE

DEVIL AND ALL

BY JOHN COLLIER

1934

Possession of Angela Bradshaw

The Right Side

Half way to Hell

After the Ball

The Devil, George, and Rosie

Hell hath no Fury

NONESUCH PRESS

PLATE 45 A somewhat stilted attempt at modernism by Francis Meynell.

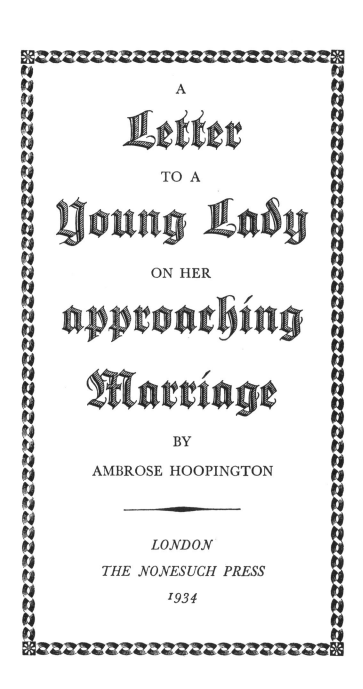

A

Letter

TO A

Young Lady

ON HER

approaching

Marriage

BY

AMBROSE HOOPINGTON

LONDON
THE NONESUCH PRESS
1934

PLATE 46 A shaded blackletter typeface by Rudolf Koch perfectly matched with a shaded border ornament from the Monotype repertoire.

THE GREEK
PORTRAIT

AN ANTHOLOGY OF ENGLISH VERSE TRANSLATIONS

FROM THE GREEK POETS (HOMER TO MELEAGER)

WITH THE CORRESPONDING

GREEK TEXT

LONDON

THE NONESUCH PRESS

ILLUSTRATED BY MARIETTE LYDIS

EDITED BY GEORGE ROSTREVOR HAMILTON

1934

PLATE 47   Set in Van Krimpen's Lutetia font.

THE CONFESSIONS OF
J.J. ROUSSEAU
IN AN ANONYMOUS
ENGLISH VERSION
FIRST PUBLISHED IN
TWO PARTS IN 1783
& 1790 NOW REVISED
AND COMPLETED BY
A. S. B. GLOVER WITH
AN INTRODUCTION
BY HAVELOCK ELLIS
ORNAMENTED WITH
WOOD-ENGRAVINGS
BY REYNOLDS STONE
VOLUME I · BOOKS I-VII
LONDON·MCMXXXVIII
THE NONESUCH PRESS

PLATE 48   Title lettered by Reynolds Stone, combining well with Eric Gill's Perpetua typeface.

In Memoriam

by Alfred Lord Tennyson

1933

London: The Nonesuch Press

PLATE 49   Blado italic type with ornaments from a somewhat later historical source.

Pope's Own Miscellany

Being a reprint of *Poems on Several Occasions* 1717 containing new poems by Alexander Pope and others

EDITED BY NORMAN AULT

London : The Nonesuch Press
MCMXXXV

PLATE 50 Set in the "Fell" types.

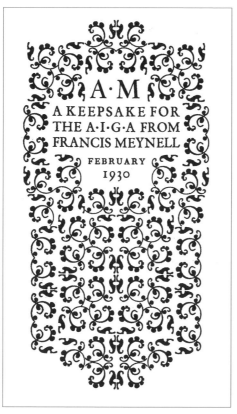

PLATE 51

A novel use of old-fashioned ornaments.

PHOTO BY JAMES L. WEIL

GIOVANNI MARDERSTEIG

Giovanni Mardersteig has been called the finest printer of the twentieth century by many of the leading typographers throughout the world. He was born Hans Mardersteig in Weimar, Germany, on 8 January 1892. Early on he developed a passion for books, but his father insisted on his studying law to ensure a reasonable livelihood. While pursuing his law studies, Mardersteig followed through on one of his interests by also studying art history. In 1919, after graduation, he persuaded publisher Kurt Wolff to start a periodical on art called *Genius*. Mardersteig quickly became dissatisfied with the level of craftsmanship he was able to achieve with this and other book projects, so he decided to start a private press with a friend, Mauro Vasetta (who soon dropped out of the venture for health reasons), in order to try to attain his goals for a well-made book.

Mardersteig could not have foreseen at that time that the Officina Bodoni was to be one of the longest operating private presses ever, lasting over fifty-five years under his direction. By comparison, The Doves Press lasted eighteen years, The Bremer Presse twenty-eight years, and The Kelmscott Press a mere seven years. Not only in longevity, but in quality, the Officina Bodoni reached superlative heights.

Vasetta was able to secure permission from the Italian government to cast several of the types of Giambattista Bodoni from the original matrices still preserved in Parma. The original Bodoni types have much more life and elegance than the many imitations which are available today under the appellation of "Bodoni." Only the handcut version produced by the Bauer typefoundry and the digitized version of three different sizes of the authentic Bodoni fonts made by International Typeface Corporation in the 1990s come even close to the original designs.

All the Officina Bodoni books were printed in Bodoni's types until Frederic Warde and Mardersteig collaborated on the first books printed in Warde's new Arrighi and Vicenza types (1926). The last major book printed in the Bodoni fonts was also the first of many Officina Bodoni books with original illustrations: Gabriele d'Annunzio's *L'Oleandro* (1936, plate 53) contains twenty-seven lithographs by Gunter Böhmer. The images swirl around the margins of the page – sometimes across the double-page spread – perfectly complementing the italic type, much the same way that Pierre Bonnard's lithographs complement the Garamond italic type in the ground-breaking 1900 Vollard edition of *Parallèlement*.

In the early days of the Officina Bodoni, Mardersteig handset and handprinted the books himself; later, compositors and pressmen were trained by Mardersteig to assist with the work. By this point Mardersteig had already achieved an enviable reputation.

He developed a warm relationship with Stanley Morison (see pp. 54–69), for whom he was to print several important books, and to whom he dedicated his lovely *Pietro Bembo On Aetna*, published in 1969, two years after Morison's death.

In 1926, the Italian government held a competition to print the complete works of Gabriele d'Annunzio. Mardersteig's name was submitted by Arnoldo Mondadori, an established Veronese printer, and he won the competition. He moved his press from Montagnola, Switzerland, to Verona, Italy, to be closer to d'Annunzio, who lived near Lake Garda. Mardersteig was to remain in Verona the rest of his life, assimilating the best of Italy's cultural heritage and changing his name to the Italian form Giovanni. The mixture of meticulous German craftsmanship and warm Italian verve resulted in the best of both of worlds in Mardersteig's work.

For the forty-seven volumes of d'Annunzio's works Mardersteig stated his intention to achieve a variety in the typographic layout, while still using just one series of types (he employed only the original Bodoni fonts), so that each volume would be part of the whole. The myriad results he was able to achieve in printing d'Annunzio's poetry, plays, prose, and non-fiction – using a mere four text sizes (and not many more display sizes) – are remarkable.

Starting in 1929, Mardersteig turned some of his energies to type design, the first fruit of which was the Griffo type, based on the letter cut by Francesco Griffo for Aldus Manutius. Next came the Zeno (1931, plate 59), which is based on the roman calligraphy of Arrighi. Fontana (1935, plate 58), Pacioli (1954), and Dante (1954) followed. All his types with the exception of Fontana were originally cut by hand by Charles Malin, the punchcutter who had previously cut the pilot size of Eric Gill's Perpetua typeface for Stanley Morison at Monotype. Dante is particularly important because the excellent version released for machine composition by the Monotype Corporation in 1955 has since been used by many fine printers. Mardersteig's Dante type, Frederic Warde's Arrighi italic, Bruce Rogers's Centaur, Eric Gill's Joanna, and Joseph Blumenthal's Emerson are the only types which were originally cut for private press use and later released for machine composition.

Nearly 200 editions were produced at the Officina Bodoni between 1923 and 1977, almost all limited to less than 500 copies. The "Editiones Officina Bodoni" were often selected and edited by Mardersteig himself; the books were always designed and overseen by him (with the possible exception of Plato's *Crito*, which may have been designed by Frederic Warde) using the finest papers and bindings, as well as presswork which extols the beauty of lovely types on sumptuous paper. Often a small part of the edition was printed on vellum.

In 1949, Mardersteig opened a small machine printing operation called the

"Stamperia Valdonega," equipped with Monotype casters and automatic Heidelberg presses. Here he was able to employ a larger array of production methods and extend his skills across a wider range of printed materials. The presswork, composition, and design accomplishments of this shop rose to the pinnacle of modern printing art, just as the work of the Officina Bodoni set the standard for handpress printing. Of course the much greater capacity and larger press runs of the machine operation meant that the books designed by Mardersteig and originating from there have reached a far wider audience than the handpress editions, though perhaps their full impact is not as well appreciated. Through the Stamperia Valdonega Mardersteig produced books on a wide variety of subjects – from verse (such as Ovid's *Metamorphoses* for The Limited Editions Club, plate 61) and *belle lettres* through scholarly monographs and commercially published volumes (such as plate 56) – for a large assortment of publishers around the world. Books were printed for old friends such as Kurt Wolff (later active in America at Pantheon Books), New Directions, Faber and Faber, Tammaro de Marinis, and others for whom Mardersteig had printed books at the Officina Bodoni, as well as numerous new clients, including several trade publishers such as Insel Verlag in Germany and Edizioni Poliphili in Italy. Giovanni Mardersteig produced eighteen volumes for the New York-based Limited Editions Club from 1931 (the year after its first series) through 1972 (five years before his death, and at a time of transition for the publisher). The first of these volumes (*The Little Flowers of Saint Francis of Assisi*, plate 55) and the next several titles were planned at the Officina Bodoni, but had to be printed at a larger establishment in order to meet the need for 1,500 copies for subscribers (which was too large a run to print on the handpress, especially considering that each title usually ran to several hundred pages). After 1949 all the work on The Limited Editions Club titles was performed at Mardersteig's Stamperia Valdonega. The basic aesthetic principles remained consistent at both shops: a small range of re-cut historical typefaces (or original typefaces historically inspired), arranged in a symmetrical, traditional manner (but never a totally allusive layout or didactic copying of an early style), with the highest standard in presswork, imposition, and other details of fine bookmaking. Monotype Bembo and his own Dante design were Mardersteig's favorite typefaces, followed by Garamond, Baskerville, and Centaur. Within these parameters, which may appear somewhat limited, he was able to achieve a variety and vitality that made him an acknowledged master of book design. Take, for example, the bold use of color stemming from the illuminated manuscript tradition, as seen in *La Gallica Historia di Drusillo*, or the title page and twenty-five hand-colored capitals in *Alphabetum*

Romanum (plate 57), both displaying a colorful verve which sets these books apart from standard traditional fare.

Though usually reticent about his work, Mardersteig was persuaded to allow his books to be exhibited at the Plantin Moretus Museum in Antwerp in 1954. Several more exhibitions followed, including shows of his work at the British Museum, the Trivulziana in Milan, and the Newberry Library in Chicago. In 1992, The Grolier Club in New York held a retrospective exhibition of Mardersteig's work to mark the centenary of his birth. (The Grolier Club exhibition included his work at the Stamperia Valdonega, in addition to examples from the Officina Bodoni.) An extensive bibliography prepared by Hans Schmoller was published in 1980. Mardersteig received many awards, including the AIGA medal in 1968 and the first Gutenberg Prize from the city of Mainz, also in 1968. He died on 27 December 1977, at the age of 85.

The Stamperia Valdonega is thriving today under the leadership of Giovanni's son, Martino, who has installed offset equipment to complement the letterpress resources; the Officina Bodoni also continues operation under Martino and his wife, Gabriella.

*

When the Second World War – which had shattered the lives of so many around the world, but particularly in Europe – ended, Morison was keen to get in touch with two of his friends and colleagues on the continent, to see how they fared after those terrible years of conflict. They found the world a different place, yet they were all able to continue to produce important work after 1945. Still, in those dreary days following the end of the War, things did not always look too rosy. Morison related this situation to Mardersteig in a letter of 9 August 1951, in which he lamented that "nothing done by the Corporation . . . since the war has afforded me any pleasure or satisfaction . . . much of this I have explained to Van Krimpen."

Van Krimpen was another designer, like Mardersteig, to whom Morison felt close – both personally and professionally. He also practiced a clear, rational style in his book design – one rooted in classical traditions, but which could not be mistaken for anything but a twentieth-century aesthetic. Both Mardersteig (with Dante) and Van Krimpen (with Lutetia, Spectrum, and Romulus) would have their typefaces cut for machine composition by the British Monotype Corporation under Morison's guidance as typographical advisor. Yet type design represented a far larger portion of Van Krimpen's work compared with Mardersteig's, whose energies were devoted mainly to the making of fine editions on the hand press, and later to a wider range of book typography on machine equipment.

SONGS

from

*SHAKESPEARE'S
PLAYS*

MDCCCCLXXIIII

VERONA

PLATE 52   Set entirely in Giovanni Mardersteig's Dante italic type.

L'imagine di me nell'acque amavi.
Dell'amore di me arsi inclinata,
sì bella nel ninfale specchio fui.
Io fui Cyane azzurra come l'aria.
Tu mi ghermisti fra natanti foglie.
L'ombra divina mi trasfigurò.
Un fiore subitaneo s'aperse
tra i miei ginocchi. Vincolata fui
da verdi intrichi, fra radici pallide
come i miei piedi, con segreto gelo.
Il sol divino mi trasfigurò.
Anelli innumerevoli alle dita
furonmi i raggi, pettini ai capelli,
monili al collo, e veste tutta d'oro.
O Aretusa, perché non ho il tuo nome?
Nascesti tu nell'isola d'Ortigia
come l'amor del violento fiume?
La Sirena scagliosa abbeveravi,
già fatto il vespero, al tacer dei flauti.
Diedi io le canne ai flauti dei pastori.
Io fui Cyane azzurra come l'aria.
L'acqua sorgiva mi restò negli occhi;
la lenta correntia mi levigò.

12

PLATE 53 Illustrations by Gunter Böhmer for d'Annunzio's *L'Oleandro.*

O Glauco, ti sovvien della Sicilia
bella?» Ed io più non vidi la grande Alpe,
il bianco mare. Io dissi: «Andiamo, andiamo!»

«Ti sovvien della bella Doriese
nomata Siracusa nell'effigie
d'oro co' suoi delfini e i suoi cavalli,
serto del mare? Noi scoprimmo un giorno,
stando su l'Acradina, la triere
che recava da Ceo l'Ode novella
di Bacchilide al re vittorioso.
Udivasi nel vento il suon del flauto
che regolava l'impeto dei remi,
or sì or no s'udiva il canto roco
del celeùste; ma silenziosa
l'Ode, foggiata di parole eterne,
più lieve che corona d'oleastro,
onerava di gloria la carena.
Scendemmo al porto. Ti sovvien dell'ora?
Un rogo era l'Acropoli in Ortigia;
ardevano le nubi su 'l Plemmirio
belle come le statue su 'l fronte
dei templi; parea teso dalla forza

13

LE RIME
DI SER GARZO
DALL'INCISA

OFFICINA BODONI
VERONA

PLATE 54 An unusual rule border design.

the salvation of his soul, set out one day and returned to St Fran‑
cis, whom he thus addressed : "Father, the convent is founded at
Bologna, send other brothers there to keep it up and reside there,
as I can no longer be of any use; indeed, I fear that the too great
honours I receive might make me lose more than I could gain."
Now St Francis, having heard, one after another, all the things
which the Lord had wrought through Brother Bernard, rendered
thanks to God, who thus began to spread abroad the poor disci‑
ples of the Cross; then sent he others of the brethren to Bologna,
and to Lombardy, and these founded many convents in divers
countries.

CHAPTER VI

HOW ST FRANCIS, WHEN ABOUT TO DIE, BLESSED THE HOLY BROTHER BERNARD, NAMING HIM VICAR OF THE ORDER

THE holiness of Brother Bernard shone forth so brightly,
that St Francis held him in great reverence, and often was
heard to praise him. One day, as St Francis was in prayer, it
was revealed to him by God that Brother Bernard, by divine per‑
mission, would sustain many painful combats with the devil. Now
St Francis felt great compassion for Brother Bernard, whom he
loved as a son; wherefore he wept and prayed for many days, im‑
ploring the Lord Jesus Christ to give him the victory over the evil
one. As he was praying thus devoutly, the Lord answered his
prayer, and said to him: "Fear not, Francis, for all the temptations
which will assail Brother Bernard are permitted by God, to in‑
crease his virtue and win for him a crown of merit; for at length
he will gain the victory over all his enemies, because he is one of
the ministers of the kingdom of heaven." This answer to prayer

19

PLATE 55   Text page in the Pastonchi type from *The Little Flowers of Saint Francis of Assisi.* New York:
The Limited Editions Club, 1930.

 questa relazione sulle linee fondamentali dell'umanesimo italiano devo premettere una breve confessione e apologia. L'argomento della relazione di gran lunga eccede la mia competenza, che non è di studioso dell'Umanesimo, ma è di studioso della letteratura italiana in genere, con un maggiore interesse per il tardo Quattro e il primo Cinquecento. Inoltre la mia competenza, quale che sia, non è aggiornata: è frutto di studi che per forza maggiore sono stati da alcun tempo interrotti. In tali condizioni avrei dovuto, come già avevo fatto di altro tema propostomi, rifiutare questo. Ma, a parte ogni altra considerazione e tentazione, ho poi pensato che ad una accolta di specialisti, gli stessi limiti e dubbi e impedimenti miei avrebbero potuto fornire materia di discussione non inutile, indicare qualche difficoltà imprevista nel trapasso dalla specializzazione alla divulgazione, dalla storia propria dell'Umanesimo, inteso come rivoluzione del pensiero e della cultura in Europa, alla storia di esso come momento della letteratura italiana. Anche ho pensato che un pubblico esame di coscienza relativo a un trentennio di studi potesse avere un interesse non soltanto individuale.

Il primo risultato di un tale esame è per me questo: che trent'anni fa, iniziando il corso dei miei studi, mi sarei sentito naturalmente inetto a discorrere delle linee fondamentali dell'umanesimo italiano, ma non avrei dubitato affatto che se ne potesse discorrere; oggi mi tocca fare i conti anche con un tale dubbio. Dirò di

7

PLATE 56   Text page from *Discorso sull'umanesimo Italiano,* Verona: Officina Bodoni, 1956.

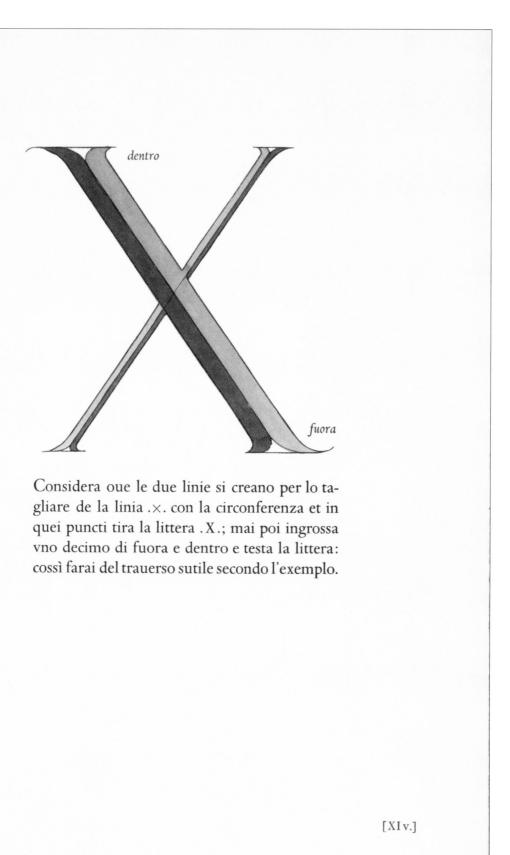

Considera oue le due linie si creano per lo ta-
gliare de la linia .×. con la circonferenza et in
quei puncti tira la littera .X.; mai poi ingrossa
vno decimo di fuora e dentro e testa la littera:
cossì farai del trauerso sutile secondo l'exemplo.

[XI v.]

PLATE 57 From *Alphabetum Romanum* by Felice Feliciano. Verona: Officina Bodoni, 1960.

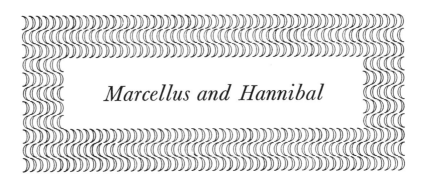

Marcellus and Hannibal

*Claudius Marcellus, the conqueror of Sicily, was killed
in a skirmish with Hannibal's troops in 208 B.C.
Hannibal said of him that he was a good
soldier but a bad general.*

HANNIBAL. Could a Numidian horseman ride no faster?
Marcellus! ho! Marcellus! He moves not . . . he is dead. Did
he not stir his fingers? Stand wide, soldiers . . . wide, forty
paces . . . give him air . . . bring water . . . halt! Gather those
broad leaves, and all the rest, growing under the brush-
wood . . . unbrace his armor. Loose the helmet first . . . his
breast rises. I fancied his eyes were fixed on me . . . they have
rolled back again. Who presumed to touch my shoulder?
This horse? It was surely the horse of Marcellus! Let no
man mount him. Ha! ha! the Romans too sink into luxury: here is gold about the charger.

GAULISH CHIEFTAIN. Execrable thief! The golden chain
of our king under a beast's grinders! The vengeance of the
gods has overtaken the impure . . .

HANNIBAL. We will talk about vengeance when we have
entered Rome, and about purity among the priests, if they
will hear us. Sound for the surgeon. That arrow may be
extracted from the side, deep as it is . . . The conqueror of
Syracuse lies before me . . . Send a vessel off to Carthage.
Say Hannibal is at the gates of Rome . . . Marcellus, who
stood alone between us, fallen. Brave man! I would rejoice
and can not . . . How awfully serene a countenance! Such

15

PLATE 58   Geometrical ornaments designed by Mardersteig from *Imaginary Conversations*.
New York: The Limited Editions Club, 1936.

SAINT MATTHEW

said unto him, Before the cock crow, thou shalt deny me thrice. And he went out, and wept bitterly.

CHAPTER XXVII

When the morning was come, all the chief priests and elders of the people took counsel against Jesus to put him to death: and when they had bound him, they led him away, and delivered him to Pontius Pilate the governor.

Then Judas, which had betrayed him, when he saw that he was condemned, repented himself and brought again the thirty pieces of silver to the chief priests and elders, saying, I have sinned in that I have betrayed the innocent blood. And they said, What is that to us? see thou to that. And he cast down the pieces of silver in the temple, and departed, and went and hanged himself. And the chief priests took the silver pieces, and said, It is not lawful for to put them

99

PLATE 59 From the Officina Bodoni edition of *The Four Gospels* in Zeno type, 1962.

Del corpo spherico la sua formatione. Capitulo LVI.
[64v.]

LA sphera per molti è stata diffinita che cosa la sia, maxime da Dionisio degno mathematico. Pure el nostro auctore con summa brevità in lo suo 11° la descrive, e quella tal descriptione da tutti posteriori se aduci, dove lui dici così: el vestigio del mezzo cerchio fa la sphera.

SPHERA fia quel che contene el vestigio de l'arco de la circumferentia del mezzo circhio. Ogni volta e in qualunche modo se prenda el semicirculo, fermando la linea del diametro, se volti atorno el dicto arco fin tanto che retorni al luogo donde se comenzò a movere: cioè facto el semicirculo sopra qual voi linea, fermando quella, el dicto semicirculo se meni atorno con tutta sua revolutione. Quel tal corpo che così fia descripto, se chiama sphera, del quale el centro fia el centro del dicto semicirculo così circumducto.

XLI

Demostratione de dicta diffinitione.

COMMO sia el semicirculo .c. facto sopra la linea .ab., facto centro el ponto .e., e tutto l'arco suo sia la parte de la circumferentia .adb. Dico che fermando la dicta linea .ab., qual fia diametro de dicto semicirculo, e quello [65r.] sopra lei circumducendo

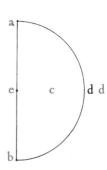

107

PLATE 60   Text page from the Officina Bodoni edition of *Da Divina Proportione* by Luca de Pacioli, 1956.

OVID'S
METAMORPHOSES

IN FIFTEEN BOOKS

★

TRANSLATED
INTO ENGLISH VERSE UNDER
THE DIRECTION OF SIR SAMUEL GARTH
BY JOHN DRYDEN, ALEXANDER POPE,
JOSEPH ADDISON, WILLIAM CONGREVE
AND OTHER EMINENT
HANDS

★

PRINTED FOR THE
MEMBERS OF THE LIMITED EDITIONS CLUB
AT THE OFFICINA BODONI IN VERONA
1958

PLATE 61   Title page in Bruce Rogers's Centaur type. One of the finest examples of Renaissance classicism.

PHOTO COURTESY OF THE MELBERT B. CARY, JR. GRAPHIC ARTS COLLECTION, RIT

Jan van Krimpen came to book design and typography through an involvement with contemporary poetry and literature. He was born on 12 January 1892, four days after Mardersteig. Early in his career he was engaged in bookbinding and calligraphy professionally, but it was his first typeface design, Lutetia (1924), that brought his work to the attention of the wider international fine printing community.

The origins of the Lutetia design are unusual. Since 1922, Van Krimpen had created the lettering for several Dutch postage stamps, which were being printed at the venerable printing house of Johannes Enschedé en Zonen in Haarlem, the Netherlands. In addition to being one of the country's leading printing firms, with an international clientele, Enschedé was also one of the two largest type foundries in Holland. Through the lettering on these postage stamps, Van Krimpen's skill in rendering letterforms came to the attention of Dr. Enschedé, who initiated the design by Van Krimpen of a roman typeface, later christened "Lutetia" in honor of the Latin name for the city of Paris. Here the font was first shown at the *Exposition Internationale des Arts Décoratifs et Industriels Modernes*. The type was awarded the Grand Prix at the exposition – quite an auspicious beginning for the rookie thirty-three-year-old designer.

The italic, which followed in 1927, shortly after the roman, is an especially graceful design, with a beautiful complement of swash characters. A few can be seen to their best advantage in *A Selection of Types* published by the Enschedé foundry, with design by Van Krimpen, in 1930 (plates 64 and 70). The restraint used in employing only four of the available swash forms (A, H, T, and Y) is indicative of his refined taste.

In 1925, the year after Lutetia, Van Krimpen joined the Enschedé firm. Among his responsibilities there, during his more than three-decade association with the company, was the designing of many books, several of which were the most important of his career. From the presses at Enschedé came his book designs for The Limited Editions Club in New York, Peter Davies in London, and the Pegasus Press in Paris, as well as for numerous Dutch publishing houses. Van Krimpen's first book design for the New York-based Limited Editions Club was the *Iliad* of Homer (plate 66), set in his Romanée font – its first use in an American book and printed at Enschedé in 1931. At the time, the intention was for Romanée to accompany a sixteenth-century italic by Christoffel Van Dijck, for which Enschedé had the original matrices, but for which the companion roman had been lost. Almost two decades later, in 1949, Van Krimpen designed a new italic to pair with Romanée roman in place of the sixteenth-century original, but this new italic, too, does not mix well with its mate. Despite this, Van

Krimpen often used Romanée to great advantage, mostly avoiding mixing the roman and italic in the same line. For example, for The Limited Editions Club *Iliad* the sixteenth-century italic is used on several pages for the introduction, while the main text is entirely in Van Krimpen's noble Romanée roman. The result is that both types look handsome, but do not appear on the same page. Another case is a selection of three poems by Richard Crashaw, published in 1930 as one of a series of books printed as Christmas keepsakes for Enschedé. In this twenty-four-page book, set in Romanée roman, italic type is only used for thirty-eight short words, indicating the speakers in dialogue or for dedication lines. Therefore the types are never really required to mix completely within a running text. It may even be that a bit of extra differentiation in these instances is an effect in distinguishing the two speakers that has been exploited to good advantage by Van Krimpen.

Another book in the same series of holiday keepsakes, *Les Fêtes de Hollande* (1955), uses Van Krimpen's later Spectrum design. Several long titles within the main text are set in italic, as is the "Notice" at the end – in this instance with some roman mixed in for titles.

Van Krimpen's book designs, while always classical (and symmetrical), could not be categorized as allusive design. He preferred a more modern typographic style – whether the subject matter be contemporary writing or reprints of older works – most often using his own typefaces. In addition to Lutetia with its lovely italic fonts, which had a quite modern look for their time – a time when historical revivals of Garamond, Baskerville, Caslon, and such dominated the type market – Van Krimpen designed three other important text typefaces: Romanée (1928, with an italic following more than two decades later in 1949), Romulus (1931), and Spectrum (1943). Lutetia, Romulus, and Spectrum were adapted for machine composition on the Monotype system, overseen by Van Krimpen's friend Stanley Morison. In addition to those major typefaces Van Krimpen designed several other handsome fonts for Enschedé, among them Open Kapitalen (1927, plate 62) and Cancelleresca Bastarda (1934). The Open Kapitalen font can be seen in both its Roman and Greek forms combined with Lutetia and Antigone Greek in *Sappho Revocata* (plate 68), published by Peter Davies in London in 1928. Both the Open Kapitalen and Antigone Greek types made their first appearance in this volume, which was designed by Van Krimpen and printed at Enschedé.

Van Krimpen's commentary on his own type designs, *On Designing and Devising Type*, published by The Typophiles in New York, is set in the Spectrum type, perhaps his most versatile typeface design. This volume, too – like most of his finest book typography – was printed under his direct control at Enschedé.

On top of his work in typeface design, Van Krimpen also produced much hand lettering for various purposes, ranging from postage stamps to engraved plaques, along with titles, logotypes, and dust jackets in association with his work in book design. All told, his type design, lettering, and book design were firmly traditional, but he was also conscious of creating work that was of its time, not a copy of any earlier style. Like Mardersteig, Van Krimpen's work was invariably symmetrical, but also like Mardersteig he was able to achieve his own recognizable style and a wide variety within classical parameters. Most of his title pages were set all in capitals and small capitals, meticulously letterspaced. Occasionally a hand-drawn logo, or even hand-lettered title line would relieve the consistency of the all-capital fonts (such as in the edition of *Donne's Poems* shown in figure 12, Introduction). Van Krimpen's books were set entirely in one style of type, using several sizes, almost never mixing fonts. A favorite element in his work would be an open initial or titling line, using either a hand-drawn letter designed to harmonize with the font used (as in the *Iliad* and *Odyssey*) or one of his open letter typeface designs (in addition to Open Kapitalen already mentioned, Enschedé produced open capitals for Van Krimpen's Lutetia and Romulus fonts). A handsome series of decorated capitals in two sizes was drawn by Van Krimpen for the Curwen Press in London in 1929. These were used like type but actually produced by photoengraving at the firm of Emery Walker. In these letters one can see the principles of his aesthetic: even though decorative letters might be considered to be inherently ornamental and even antique, he has created a design that looks neither fussy nor old-fashioned. The crisp, clean lines of the letters, with their elegant proportions and refined drawing, make them very much of the twentieth century, even if the task at hand might at first seem to cry for an earlier look. An example of Van Krimpen's use of his own lettering in one of his designs is the large swash initial used for the opening of the *Rubáiyát of Omar Khayyám* (plate 63) printed by Enschedé for A. A. Balkema in Amsterdam.

Not only at the Curwen Press and *The Fleuron* in London, but elsewhere, Van Krimpen's work caught the attention of the finest printers and typographers. In the United States, Daniel Berkeley Updike (in 1927) and Joseph Blumenthal (in 1930) were among the first to use Lutetia in book work. On the West Coast, The Grabhorn Press also put the Lutetia type to impressive use at its shop in San Francisco within two years of its being issued. Bruce Rogers used Lutetia in one of his most important books: *Ancient Books and Modern Discoveries*, printed at Rudge for the Caxton Club of Chicago in 1927 (albeit with a substitute e, h, m, and n). A slightly revised version of Lutetia was developed by Porter Garnett for the monumental catalogue of the Frick Collection, a project which Rogers would finally bring to completion in

1949 after several other designers had started and stopped work on it. Meynell (*The Greek Portrait*, plate 47) and Tschichold (*The Golden Ass* for Penguin Books) would also use Van Krimpen typefaces in their book design work.

The effect of the combination of a sharp, crisp Van Krimpen typeface on a relatively smooth and white paper, along with highly letterspaced lines of capitals with generous amounts of white space between the lines is hard to convey. The whole gives a feeling of a light, modern look – never dark or old-fashioned. This is precisely what he was out to achieve: modernity within a classical framework. He was fortunate to have several Dutch publishers who were in agreement with his principles; contemporaries including A. M. Stols, S. H. de Roos, and A. A. Balkema supported Van Krimpen's work, commissioning him to design books which they published. Van Krimpen died suddenly while being driven to work on 20 October 1958.

While several prominent twentieth-century book designers also designed at least one text type, and most used hand-lettering to some extent, Van Krimpen's achievements in all three fields (book design, type design, and calligraphy) were rivaled only by those of Rudolf Koch and Hermann Zapf. Like Zapf later on, he believed in a firmly modern design aesthetic, using mostly contemporary typefaces (and, understandably enough, often – but not exclusively – his own) in an essentially modern manner, not a consciously historic one.

*

Van Krimpen's typographic style was truly conservative and unmistakably classical, though always with an eye towards being contemporary. He certainly would have frowned upon the radical experiments being produced in the 1920s and '30s by avant-garde typographers associated with the Bauhaus – at exactly the same time he was making his style known amongst the fine printing community in Europe and abroad. One of the foremost (if not *the* foremost) proponents of "the new typography" was a young German who was ten years his junior: Jan Tschichold. Yet, though the styles of the two Jans in the 1920s and '30s were at opposite ends of the spectrum, there may not have been quite as much of a dichotomy between them as there initially appears to be. By the Second World War, Tschichold would be producing books that in many ways follow the same principles as his elder namesake in Holland.

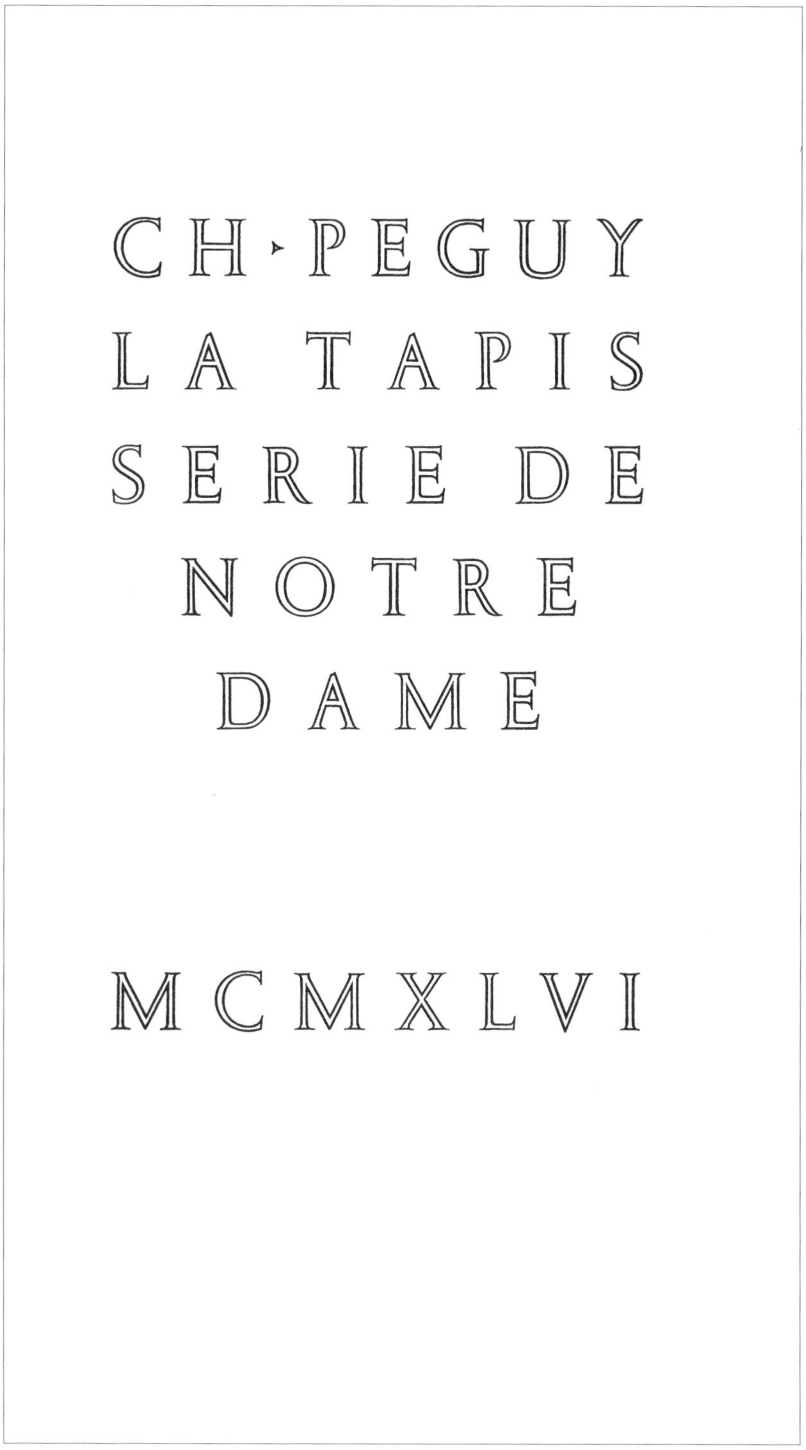

CH · PEGUY
LA TAPIS
SERIE DE
NOTRE
DAME

MCMXLVI

PLATE 62   Title page set entirely in one size of Van Krimpen's Open
Kapitalen typeface.

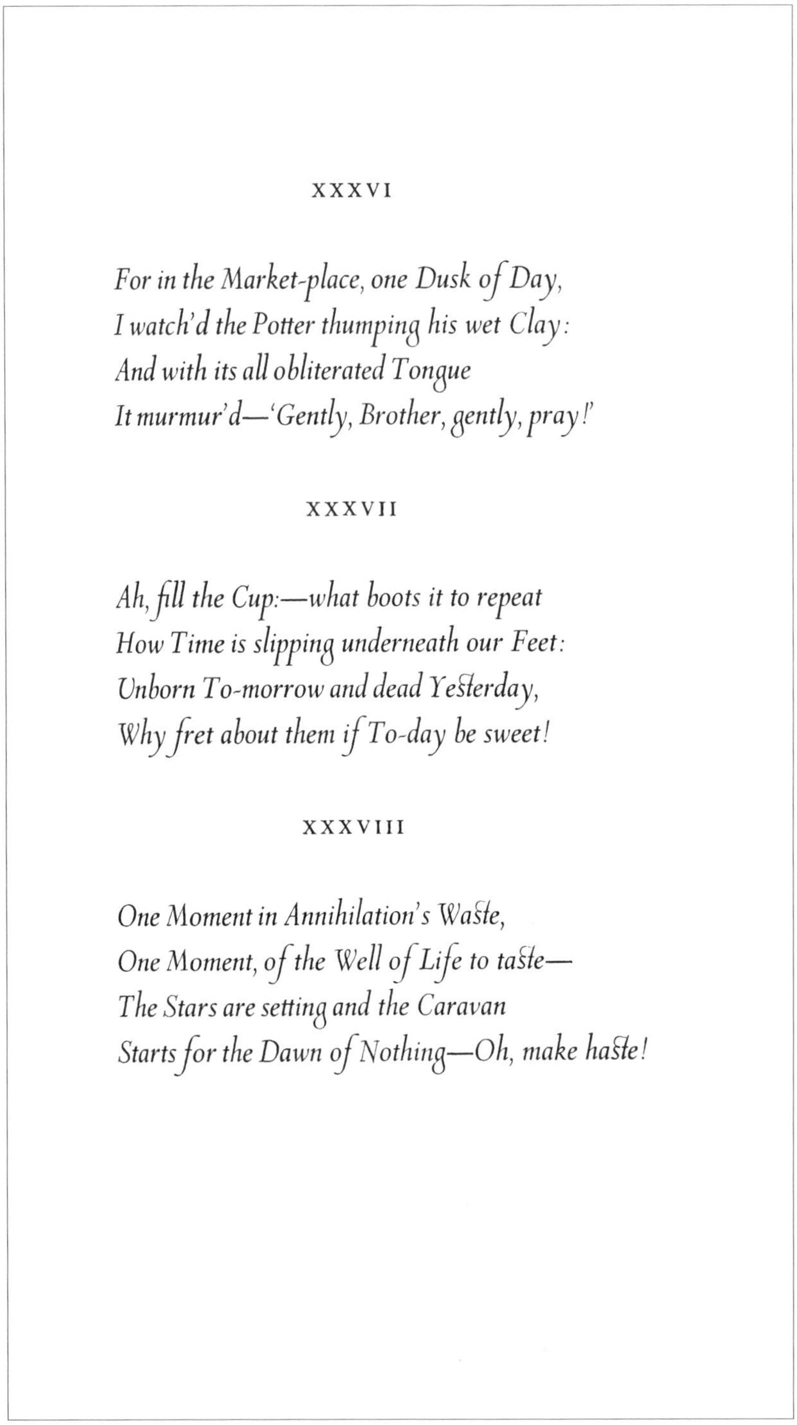

XXXVI

For in the Market-place, one Dusk of Day,
I watch'd the Potter thumping his wet Clay:
And with its all obliterated Tongue
It murmur'd—'Gently, Brother, gently, pray!'

XXXVII

Ah, fill the Cup:—what boots it to repeat
How Time is slipping underneath our Feet:
Unborn To-morrow and dead Yesterday,
Why fret about them if To-day be sweet!

XXXVIII

One Moment in Annihilation's Waste,
One Moment, of the Well of Life to taste—
The Stars are setting and the Caravan
Starts for the Dawn of Nothing—Oh, make haste!

PLATE 63 Text page from Van Krimpen's design for the *Rubáiyát of Omar Khayyám* (Amsterdam: A. A. Balkema, 1945), set in his own Cancelleresca Bastarda font.

*A
SELECTION
OF TYPES FROM
SIX CENTURIES IN
USE AT THE OFFICE OF
JOH.ENSCHEDÉ EN ZONEN
AT HAARLEM,HOLLAND
DEDICATED TO THE
FRIENDS OF THE
HOUSE
★*

PLATE 64 Type specimen book set in Van Krimpen's Lutetia types, with a restrained use of swash capitals.

128,129

PSALM CXXVIII
A SONG OF DEGREES.

BLESSED is every one that feareth the LORD; that walketh in his ways.

2. For thou shalt eat the labour of thine hands: happy shalt thou be, and it shall be well with thee.

3. Thy wife shall be as a fruitful vine by the sides of thine house: thy children like olive plants round about thy table.

4. Behold, that thus shall the man be blessed that feareth the LORD.

5. The LORD shall bless thee out of Zion: and thou shalt see the good of Jerusalem all the days of thy life.

6. Yea, thou shalt see thy children's children, and peace upon Israel.

PSALM CXXVIIII
A SONG OF DEGREES.

MANY a time have they afflicted me from my youth, may Israel now say:

2. Many a time have they afflicted me from my youth: yet they have not prevailed against me.

3. The plowers plowed upon my back: they made long their furrows.

4. The LORD is righteous: he hath cut asunder the cords of the wicked.

218

PLATE 65   Text page from *The Psalms.* Utrecht, 1947, published by S. H. De Roos.

THE ELEVENTH BOOK

THE saffron morn, with early blushes spread,
Now rose refulgent from Tithonus' bed;
With new-born day to gladden mortal sight,
And gild the courts of heaven with sacred light:
When baleful Eris, sent by Jove's command,
The torch of discord blazing in her hand,
Through the red skies her bloody sign extends,
And, wrapt in tempests, o'er the fleet descends.
High on Ulysses' bark her horrid stand
She took, and thunder'd through the seas and land.
Even Ajax and Achilles heard the sound,
Whose ships, remote, the guarded navy bound.
Thence the black fury through the Grecian throng
With horror sounds the loud Orthian song:
The navy shakes, and at the dire alarms
Each bosom boils, each warrior starts to arms.
No more they sigh, inglorious to return,
But breathe revenge, and for the combat burn.
    The king of men his hardy host inspires
With loud command, with great example fires;
Himself first rose, himself before the rest
His mighty limbs in radiant armour dress'd.
And first he cased his manly legs around
In shining greaves with silver buckles bound;
The beaming cuirass next adorn'd his breast,

289

PLATE 66   Text page from *The Iliad*. New York: The Limited Editions Club, 1931. Set in Romanée
with elegant hand-drawn initials as the only ornamentation throughout the book.

PLATE 67 Title-page spread with an ornamental border by Van Krimpen. Such decorative treatment was unusual for him.

λϝ′   εἰς Νηρηΐδας

⌈Χρύσιαι⌉ Νηρήϊδες, ἀβλάβη⌈ν μοι⌉
⌈τὸν κασί⌉γνητον δότε τυίδ' ἴκεσθαι,
⌈κᾶ μὲν⌉ ᾦ θύμῳ κε θέλη γένεσθαι,
    ⌈ταῦτα τε⌉λέσθην·

⌈ὄσσα δὲ πρ⌉όσθ' ἄμβροτε, πάντα λῦσαι,
⌈καὶ φίλοι⌉σι ϝοῖσι χάραν γένεσθαι
⌈καὶ δύαν ἔ⌉χθροισι· γένοιτο δ' ἄμμι
    ⌈δύσκλεα μ⌉ηδείς.

⌈τὰν κασιγ⌉νήταν δὲ θέλοι πόησθαι
⌈ἔμμορον⌉ τίμας· ὀνίαν δὲ λύγραν
⌈καὶ λόγοις⌉ ὄτοισι πάροιθ' ἀχεύων
    ⌈ἄμμον ἐδά⌉μνα

⌈κῆρ ὄνειδο⌉ς εἰσαΐων τό κ' ἐν χρῷ
⌈κέρρεν, ἀλ⌉λ' ἐπ' ἀγ⌈λαΐ⌉ᾳ πολίταν
⌈ἀββάλην ἄ⌉λλως, ⌈ὄτα⌉ νῆ κε δαῦτ' οὐ-
    ⌈δὲν διὰ μά⌉κρω·

⌈καὶ σύνωρ⌉ον, αἴ κ⌈ε θέλη, ἀξίοι⌉σι⌈ν⌉
⌈ἐν λέχεσσ' ἔ⌉χην· σὺ ⌈δὲ⌉, κύνν⌈'⌉ ἔ⌉ρε⌈μ⌉να,
⌈ρῖνα πρὸς γάᾳ⌉ θεμ⌈έν⌉α κακάν⌈θην⌉
    ⌈ἄλλα πεδάγρ⌉η.

20

PLATE 68   A text page from *Sappho Revocata*, set in Antigone Greek, London: Peter Davies, 1928.

111

Les œubres de

Françoys Villon

Les Lais / Le Testament
Poésies diverses
Le Jargon

Joh. Enschedé en Zonen
Harlem / Mdccccxxix

PLATE 69 Title line hand-lettered by Van Krimpen.

LIBER
ECCLESIASTES
QUI AB HEBRÆIS
COHELETH
APPELLATUR

HARLEMI
EX TYPOGRAPHIA ENSCHEDAIANA
ANNO DOMINI MDCCCCXXX

PLATE 70   Lutetia roman, from the type specimen illustrated in plate 64.

PHOTO BY B. HEGER

Jan Tschichold was born on 2 April 1902. His father was a sign painter who first exposed his son to letterforms and their arrangement. Jan studied under Hermann Delitsch at the Leipzig Academy, later taking graduate courses with two famous designers: Walter Tiemann and Hugo Steiner-Prag. He himself taught at the Academy from the age of nineteen to twenty-two.

Tschichold burst onto the typographic scene as a leading proponent (if not *the* leading proponent) of the modern asymmetric style with the publication of *elementare typographie* [*sic*] in 1925. This was followed by *Die neue Typographie*, which was to become the gospel of the movement, in 1928; and *Typographische Gestaltung* in 1935 (later translated into English under the title *Asymmetric Typography*, figure 11, Introduction). Almost all of Tschichold's book design prior to 1935 was asymmetrically arranged. In 1935, he published "Vom richtigen Satz auf Mittelachse" ("The design of centered typography") in *Typographische Monatsblätter*, No. 4, his first article acknowledging that symmetrical typography was acceptable. In the late 1930s, after nearly two decades as one of the most influential proponents of the new typography, Tschichold made an apparent about-face and abruptly began professing a rigidly classic, symmetrical style.

Much – perhaps too much – has been said about Tschichold's well-known conversion from a pioneer of the modern typographic movement to his strict adherence to the traditional symmetric style in the arrangement of type. Max Bill asserted in *Schweizer Graphische Mitteilungen* that Tschichold was a renegade from his own teaching. As Ruari McLean noted, "Tschichold has been criticized because he preached a revolutionary gospel, then changed his mind and returned to convention." An article in *Modern Graphic Design* accused Tschichold of turning "his back on the philosophy and work which brought him admiration and acclaim." Many from Tschichold's own camp, like Max Bill, were to feel betrayed by one of their leaders, while the conservative typographic elite, such as Morison, Updike, et al., were cautious to welcome him as a convert to their aesthetic.

Tschichold's own explanation of the immediate reason for his change of style comes from an unexpected quarter. He likens "the new typography" to National Socialism (Nazism) and Fascism, seeing "obvious similarities . . . in the ruthless restrictions of typefaces, a parallel to Goebbels's infamous political alignment, and the more or less military arrangement of the lines." Tschichold did not want to be "guilty of spreading the very ideas which caused him to leave Germany." One might suspect that other, more aesthetic reasons entered into the conversion.

It is fairly obvious that Tschichold was deeply upset by his harsh treatment at the hands of the Nazis. In 1933, after establishing himself as a leader in his field, and teaching at respected institutions in Germany for twelve years (his entire adult life up to that time), he was arrested. He soon left Germany for Basle, Switzerland, where he was to live for most of his remaining days (with the notable exception of a few years in England reforming the typography of Penguin Books, plates 74, 75, and 78). The blow to his self-esteem, let alone his career and position as a noted authority, must have been tremendous for such a proud and vocal man. One can see how someone as dogmatic as he would react strongly against all he once held as true – among which was a belief in German typographic eminence and "die neue Typographie."

Tschichold wrote "so many things in [*Die neue Typographie*] are erroneous because my experience was so small" and, "today I do not entirely agree with statements [I made in *Typographische Gestaltung*], no matter how effective they have been as a basis for the creation of a new style. The harsh rejection of the previous style, however, is the condition for the creation of a different one." Perhaps one can detect in these statements some reaction to Tschichold's treatment by the Nazis, or even a rationalizing of the polar extremes his typographic philosophy was to espouse.

However, astute observers have noticed that any dichotomy in Tschichold's work may not be as polar as it appears on the surface. Noel Martin, in his introduction to a catalogue of Tschichold's work, has written that "those who find his later work antiquated have looked only superficially," and Hans Peter Willberg wrote, "it seems to me that in fact the early and later Tschichold are not so far apart: both had the same aims: it was just how they achieved them that was different. The aims were clarity, order, transparency of meaning, simplicity in design." This was, indeed, the case. A comparison of Tschichold's early writings, when he was an outspoken proponent of the new typography, and his later articles elucidating his views on the beauty of classical typography, reveal many similarities showing up amongst the oft-noted differences. For example, no one would be surprised that he wrote in one of his later publications, "capitals should always be letterspaced. Their letterspaces should be carefully well-balanced by the use of several different sorts in accordance with their optical value." However, in a much earlier book, written during his Bauhaus period, *Asymmetric Typography*, Tschichold wrote "faultless letter-spacing [of capitals] to achieve an even rhythm is absolutely necessary."

Of particular interest from the earlier period of Tschichold's conversion to classical typography (from about 1933 to 1950) are his designs for fifty-three volumes in the Birkhäuser Classic series (including a ten-volume Shakespeare and a twelve-volume

Goethe) for the Basle publisher between 1933 and 1945; and about 500 books for Penguin Books in London in a mere twenty-nine months from 1947 to 1949. In these volumes he maintained his careful attention to the spacing of letters and lines of type, rational imposition of all elements on the page, and attention to the small details of bookmaking – all within a strictly limited budget, proving beyond any doubt that a good typographer is more important to successful book design than the expense lavished on the production.

Tschichold grew to regret his early belief that sans-serif types were the proper vehicle for modern writing. *Die neue Typographie* was set in sans-serif, but surprisingly *Typographische Gestaltung* is set in a serif type (Bodoni), with a slab-serif font (City) being employed for the headlines. All of Tschichold's later books were, of course, set in traditional serif types. He wrote, "it was a juvenile opinion to consider the sans-serif as the most suitable or even the most contemporary type face. A typeface has first to be legible, or rather readable; and a sans-serif is certainly not the most legible type when set in quantity, let alone readable." What is odd, however, is that as early as 1935 in *Typographische Gestaltung* he said, "for body matter, nearly all the classical romans are suitable. Caslon is one of the most beautiful." This shows more classicism in Tschichold's early typographic dogma than is generally realized. Even more traditional is the following dictum on placement from the same book: "the type area of a novel and its placing on the page are also hard to improve," referring to the norms of classical book typography!

Tschichold's style before and after his so-called "conversion" of the mid-1940s look radically different on the surface. Surely one sees more classical types (such as Centaur, plate 73, and Caslon, plate 74), centered layouts, ornamentation (plate 74), and generally traditional typographic design after this change (plate 77). But a more comprehensive study would reveal similarities between his asymmetric and symmetric work. We could summarize these consistent elements as follows:

¶ The choice of clear, well-proportioned typefaces, whether they be serif or sans-serif types. In his later typography Garamond (plate 77), Baskerville, Bembo, Bell, and other classic roman types dominate; but even in his early period, where there is a wide selection of sans-serifs, Egyptians (plate 72), scripts, etc., the typefaces used are always scrupulously selected as among the finest of their kind. Mediocre types of any variety were avoided.

¶ Meticulous letterspacing of words set in capital letters. Tschichold was notorious as an uncompromising perfectionist regarding the spacing of words all in capitals. Whether in his title pages for Penguin Books (plate 78) or in his early film posters (plate 71), capitals are carefully spaced. In this regard there is more consistency between his early and late work than between his classical title pages and, say, D.B. Updike or Bruce Rogers, who occasionally set words in all-capitals with little or no letterspacing to achieve a specific effect.

¶ Exceptional care with the placement of various items on the page. In both his traditional and modern designs, Tschichold carefully balanced all the elements he had to work with (see plates 72 and 76). All the weights, tensions, white spaces, etc., were thoroughly considered in achieving a successful composition, whether it be symmetrically or asymmetrically arranged.

¶ Thoughtful consideration of materials. Unlike other important typographers of this century, most of Tschichold's work was on inexpensive books, not fine editions. He rarely worked with handmade papers or specially commissioned typefaces, yet whatever the limitations placed on him, he always showed sensitivity to selection of the most sympathetic materials.

¶ The use of a fairly limited palette of typefaces and elements on the page (for example, plate 72 uses three fonts only, and plate 77 employs two typefaces – Garamond in two sizes and a blackletter for the title in a larger size, while plate 78 shows only two fonts, each in one size only, highlighted by decorative rules). There is a well-known Tschichold axiom that three sizes of type are almost always sufficient. This is in keeping with the overall impression of his late work, but even as early as 1935 he wrote, "too many sizes in one job are impractical and seldom give good results."

In these key areas there is a strongly consistent streak in Tschichold's work, whether it be from 1930 or 1960. Looking deeper beneath the surface of his typography we see more similarity between early and late work than between his work and that of his contemporaries.

Tschichold's attention to these often overlooked fine points of printing set him apart from most of his peers, whether they were Bauhaus designers or traditional typographers. There is a care in spacing, balance and placement, and an unusual selection of typefaces in Tschichold's work that makes it readily identifiable as his own.

He died on 11 August 1974.

*

Perhaps Jan Tschichold's finest student was a typographer who did not limit himself to either radical asymmetry or rigid classicism. From 1938 to 1941 Max Caflisch worked at the Swiss publishing firm of Benno Schwabe & Co. in Basle, where Jan Tschichold worked part-time from 1933 until 1940. At Schwabe (in addition to work for other Swiss publishers and printers such as Benteli, the Swiss office of the Monotype Corporation, as well as one or two specialized American publishers such as The Limited Editions Club and the Imprint Society), Caflisch produced some of the finest book design of the post-war era. At these publishers, and with numerous other clients, he combined both classic and asymmetric elements in his extensive production of books, type specimens, and other printed matter.

NORMA TALMADGE
IN KiKi

PHOEBUS
PALACE

SHOWING AT . . . 400 615 830
SUNDAYS . . . 145 400 615 830

PLATE 71   An early poster design by Jan Tschichold.

Thomas Morus	. . . .	**16.** Jahrhundert
Bellamy	. . . .	**19.** Jahrhundert
Illing	. . . .	**20.** Jahrhundert

Illing

**uto-
polis**

Werner Illing

utopolis

Phantastischer Zukunftsroman

„Ein Zukunftsgemälde einer freien Gemeinschaft Utopien mit der Hauptstadt Utopolis. Von erfinderischer Phantasie mit allen technisch-mechanischen Fortschrittsmöglichkeiten ausgestattet • In vielem ist das Buch Gegenwartssatire am Stoff einer imaginär erschauten Zukunft. Illing hat Phantasie, einen einfachen, bildhaft genauen, unprätentiösen Stil und als Bestes eine gute, tatwillige Gesinnung."   Die Literatur.

In Ganzleinen gebunden 4.30 RM

PLATE 72   An early dust jacket design by Tschichold.

PLATE 73   A late dust jacket design by Tschichold, set in Bruce Rogers's Centaur type.

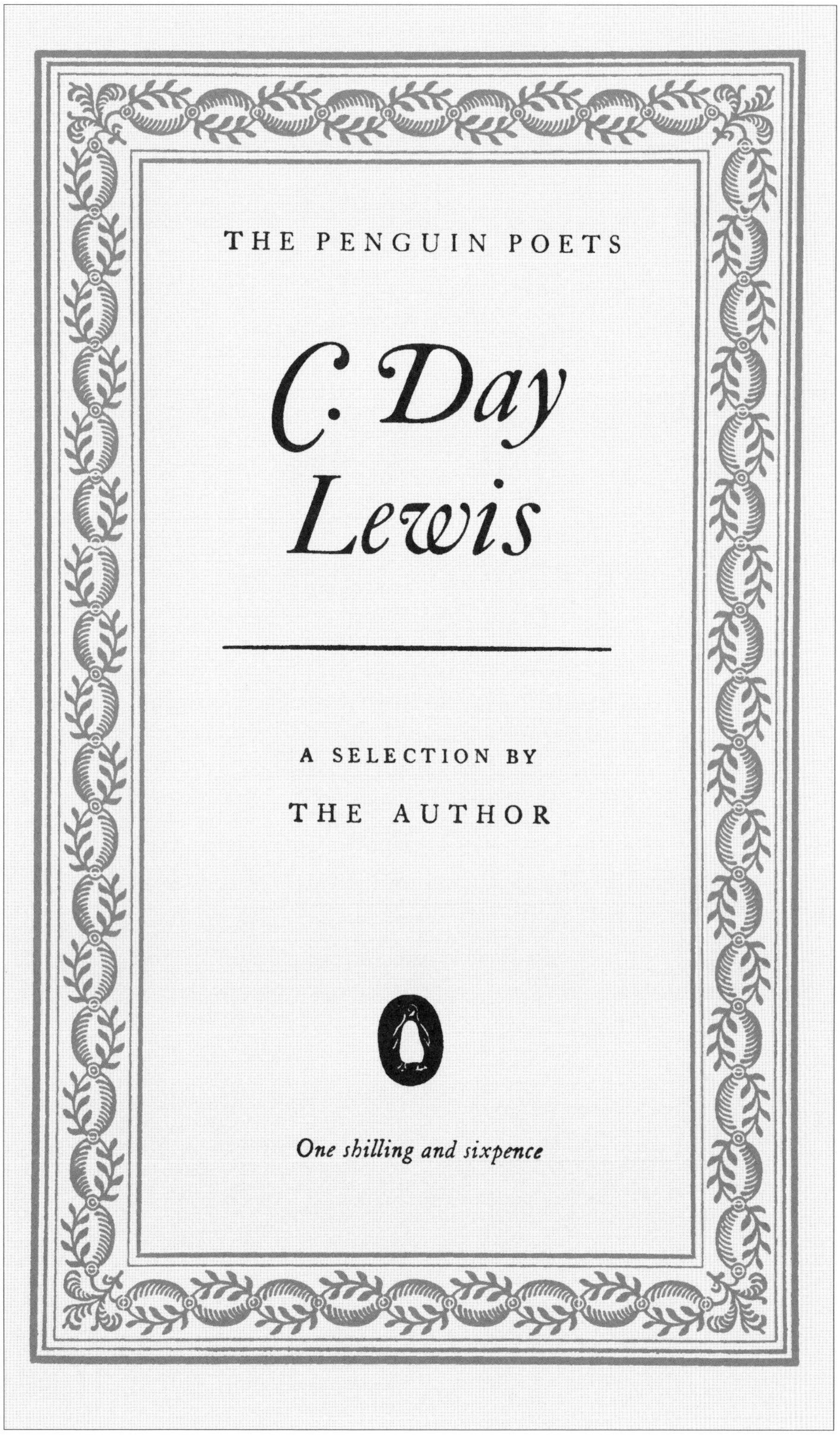

THE PENGUIN POETS

*C. Day
Lewis*

A SELECTION BY

THE AUTHOR

One shilling and sixpence

PLATE 74   Caslon type with a border made up of period ornaments.

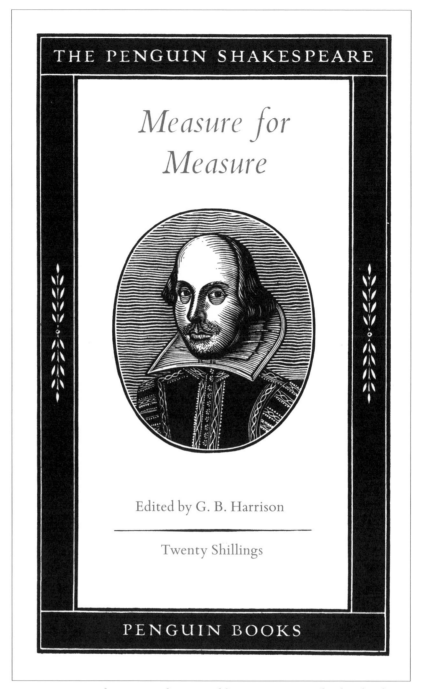

PLATE 75   Wood engraving by Reynolds Stone; typography, border design, and lettering by Tschichold.

JAN TSCHICHOLD

FORMENWANDLUNGEN

&

DER ET-ZEICHEN

PLATE 76 A study of ampersands published by the Stempel type foundry in Frankfurt, Germany.

JAN TSCHICHOLD

𝕸𝖊𝖎𝖘𝖙𝖊𝖗𝖇𝖚𝖈𝖍 𝖉𝖊𝖗 𝕾𝖈𝖍𝖗𝖎𝖋𝖙

EIN LEHRBUCH

MIT VORBILDLICHEN

SCHRIFTEN

AUS VERGANGENHEIT

UND GEGENWART

FÜR

SCHRIFTENMALER

GRAPHIKER

BILDHAUER · GRAVEURE

LITHOGRAPHEN

VERLAGSHERSTELLER

BUCHDRUCKER

ARCHITEKTEN UND

KUNSTSCHULEN

━━

OTTO MAIER · VERLAG

RAVENSBURG

PLATE 77   The German edition of this book (shown here) has the title set in a blackletter type. The English edition of this book, also designed by Tschichold and published by Van Nostrand Rheinhold, is set entirely in roman type.

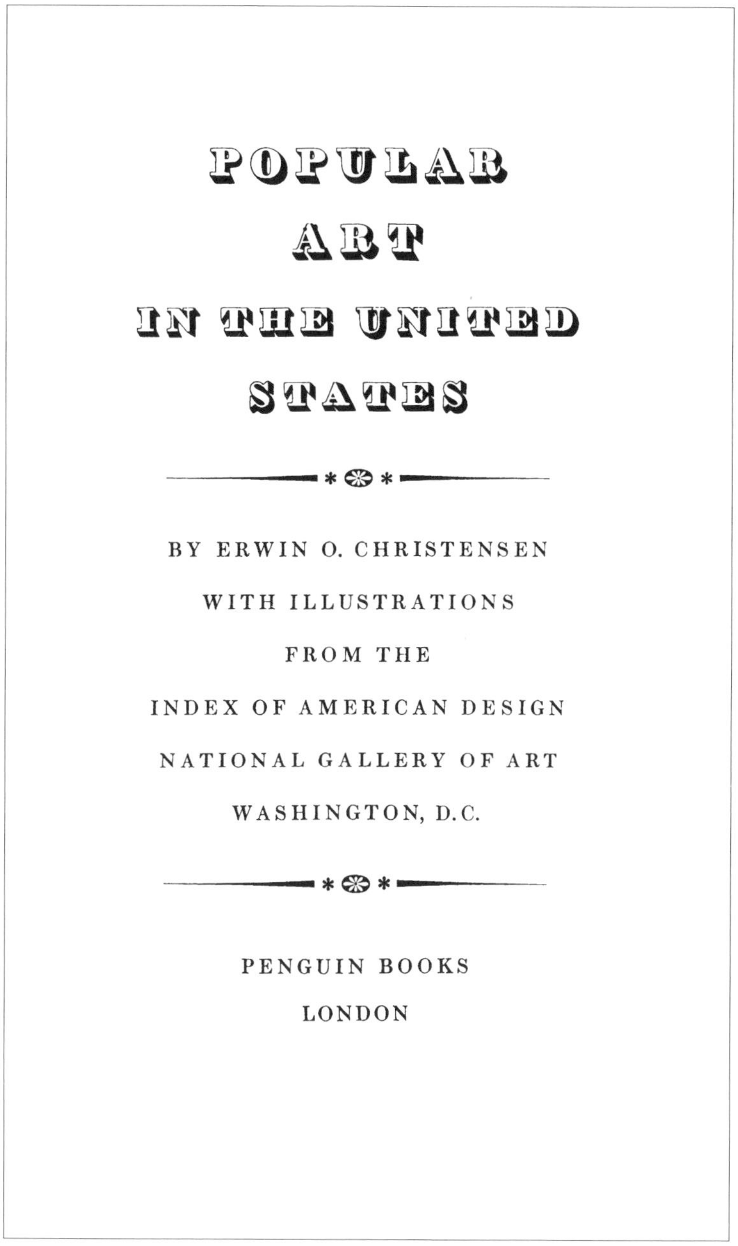

POPULAR
ART
IN THE UNITED
STATES

— * ✺ * —

BY ERWIN O. CHRISTENSEN

WITH ILLUSTRATIONS

FROM THE

INDEX OF AMERICAN DESIGN

NATIONAL GALLERY OF ART

WASHINGTON, D.C.

— * ✺ * —

PENGUIN BOOKS

LONDON

PLATE 78   One of hundreds of title pages designed by Tschichold
for Penguin Books, London.

The evolution of book design in the twentieth century can be seen as a tug-of-war between traditional and reactionary, allusive elements, and the striving for a new, modern idiom. The overwhelming majority of the book designs of Updike, Rogers, Meynell, and to a lesser extent Morison, are allusive designs – for the most part relying on revivals of earlier typefaces and historical ornamentation and layout for their effectiveness. Yet it must be added that hardly ever would any of these skilled designers create a pedantic copy of an earlier book; instead, they took elements of the past and adapted them to contemporary work and production methods, just as the type manufacturers of their era would adapt and modify fonts according to twentieth-century needs. Still the origins of the aesthetic principles in most of the finest designs of many twentieth-century typographers are clearly traceable back to earlier periods.

Various movements (often quite radical) to break away from historic precedent appeared from time to time in the twentieth century. The best known, and perhaps most successful of these movements, is often simply called "the Bauhaus," referring to the school for modern applied art established in Weimar, Germany, in the twenties, followed by a move to Dessau, and finally Berlin in the thirties. The influence of Bauhaus principles on architecture, typography, and other arts is still felt strongly today. Jan Tschichold was one of the foremost proponents – and certainly the leading voice – of Bauhaus typography, despite the fact that he was never a member of the Bauhaus school itself. However, as we have seen, for various reasons (some apparently having little to do with aesthetics), Tschichold would break completely from the modern, asymmetric style, and later in life firmly profess a devout classicism, including many allusive elements, including historical typefaces and use of ornamentation – both of which were unacceptable to the Bauhaus style.

Prominent book designers from the latter part of the century, such as de Beauclair and Zapf, would practice a typographic style relatively devoid of the allusive elements, which were so prominent in the earlier part of the century. Rarely would one see heavy ornamentation in their work, and when ornament was employed it was in a fresh and modern way. They preferred new types, while still occasionally using a font with historic origins. Both would use typographic elements rarely if ever seen in allusive book design, such as sans-serif typefaces, asymmetric layouts, and unusual modern materials and production methods.

Yet perhaps there is a middle ground between these two camps: must modern typography be ignored if one is to practice allusive typography from time to time?

And why shouldn't modern typographers be able to incorporate earlier elements into their work, even once in a while creating an almost totally allusive volume, thereby increasing the scope of their repertoire? Indeed, if we look closely enough we would see this premise of "co-existence" in the work of Van Krimpen and Mardersteig. Both were firmly classical typographers, yet they eschewed imitation of earlier styles (though for Mardersteig this was true mainly after he moved on from the exclusive use of Bodoni's types, sometime after the end of the large d'Annunzio project around 1937). Even in the work of Rogers, Meynell, and Morison, there were numerous instances of modern – even asymmetric – layouts and new typefaces. Conversely, Zapf and de Beauclair would occasionally use historical typefaces and ornamentation in their book designs. The dividing line between the camps was not too firmly drawn in the work of these eminent book designers. Only with Tschichold did there appear to be a black-and-white distinction between the two stylistic approaches. The fact that Tschichold wrote so widely on the subject of typography – promoting a complete break from historical styles early on, and later doing an about-face and professing a strict historical classicism – caused much backtracking and re-statement of principles in his later writings.

Max Caflisch, a protégé of Tschichold's born on 25 October 1916, would put the principles of these competing theories to work side-by-side in a long career spanning half the century. Allusive typography, using historic typefaces in a layout echoing an earlier style, can be seen in many examples such as a pamphlet on William Morris and the Kelmscott Press (plate 80), *Francesco Colonna und Aldo Manuzio* (1962), and Caflisch's own monograph on the sixteenth-century Granjon Arabesque, *Kleines Spiel mit Ornamenten* (1965, plate 85). A twentieth-century asymmetric style is displayed in other Caflisch designs, such as *Le Centaure* (1962), *Das höhe Lied* (1964), *Drei dutzend Fabeln von Äsop* (1967), and *Typographie braucht Schrift* (set in a sans-serif font, 1978). Still other layouts use a clear, symmetric layout which is classically inspired yet modern in feel, like much of the work of Van Krimpen and Mardersteig, for example *The Discourses of Epictetus* (1966, plate 81) and *Homo Caelestis* (plate 82).

Caflisch's use of an exceptionally wide assortment of typefaces from historical revivals such as Bembo (plate 82) and Garamond (plate 81), through sans-serif fonts such as Demos and Optima, and modern twentieth-century serif fonts such as Zapf's Marconi, Morison's Times New Roman, and his own open titling font, Columna (plate 84), all arranged in myriad ways (with neither allusive nor asymmetric layouts prevailing) gives his work a breadth which is as wide as that of any typographer of the twentieth century.

One certainly should not underestimate the accomplishments of typographers who flourished mainly in a particular mode of designing, whether it be allusive design or modern layouts, but the variety of designs employed by Caflisch shows the possibilities offered by a wide assortment of themes in book design. The key, of course, is to always find the appropriate style for the text at hand: a sixteenth-century author such as Labé is appropriately handled with Garamond types and arabesque ornamentation, while a modern author would more appropriately be set in Times New Roman or another original twentieth-century type.

*

The work of Max Caflisch is scarcely known outside a small group of aficionados of fine book typography. Perhaps this is partially because he worked mainly in a language other than English; or perhaps it is because much of his skill lies in the subtle nuances of book design that so often go unnoticed (but in some ways the same can be said of Updike, Morison, and Mardersteig). The same two factors have restricted awareness of a man who is surely one of the finest book designers of the twentieth century, yet scarcely known outside of his native Germany. Gotthard de Beauclair was a student of Rudolf Koch (1876–1934), the great German calligrapher / type designer, who worked for the Klingspor typefoundry and taught at the Offenbach Werkstatt. De Beauclair was also a co-worker of Hermann Zapf, who is discussed in the final chapter of this survey.

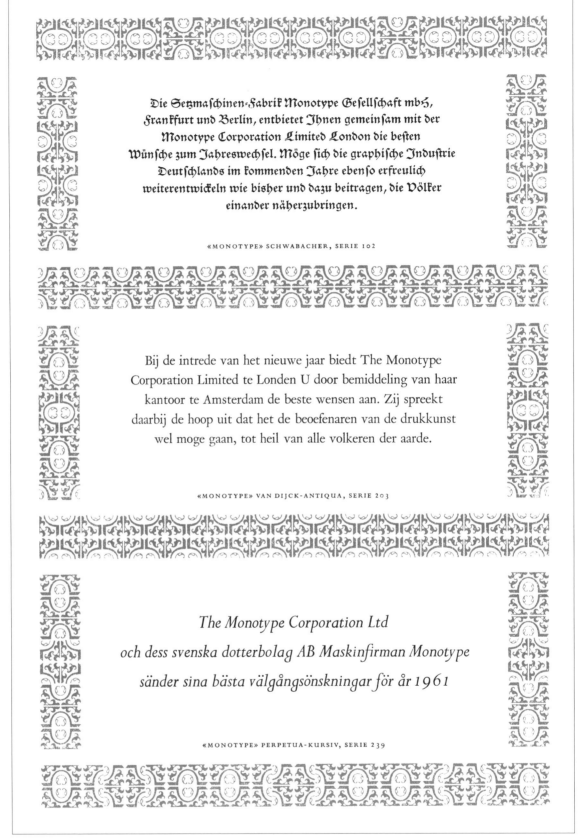

Die Setzmaschinen-Fabrik Monotype Gesellschaft mbh,
Frankfurt und Berlin, entbietet Ihnen gemeinsam mit der
Monotype Corporation Limited London die besten
Wünsche zum Jahreswechsel. Möge sich die graphische Industrie
Deutschlands im kommenden Jahre ebenso erfreulich
weiterentwickeln wie bisher und dazu beitragen, die Völker
einander näherzubringen.

«MONOTYPE» SCHWABACHER, SERIE 102

Bij de intrede van het nieuwe jaar biedt The Monotype
Corporation Limited te Londen U door bemiddeling van haar
kantoor te Amsterdam de beste wensen aan. Zij spreekt
daarbij de hoop uit dat het de beoefenaren van de drukkunst
wel moge gaan, tot heil van alle volkeren der aarde.

«MONOTYPE» VAN DIJCK-ANTIQUA, SERIE 203

The Monotype Corporation Ltd

och dess svenska dotterbolag AB Maskinfirman Monotype

sänder sina bästa välgångsönskningar för år 1961

«MONOTYPE» PERPETUA-KURSIV, SERIE 239

PLATE 79   An interesting mixture of various typefaces and ornaments from an issue of the *Monotype Newsletter*.

L faut, pour comprendre William Morris et pour mesurer l'extraordinaire influence qui fut la sienne sur toute une époque, remonter dans le temps et dans la pensée aux années victoriennes allant de 1840 à la fin du siècle. Placée dans ce cadre – et dans un tel cadre seulement – l'aventure morrissienne devient alors dans son domaine la plus surprenante épopée qui se puisse imaginer, une épopée mariant l'art et la morale, la politique et le sens de la beauté, les idéaux de la jeunesse et un effort continu vers plus de justice, une épopée culminant enfin en ces deux mots de *socialisme esthétique*, qui furent et demeurèrent la devise de William Morris sa vie durant.

Et peut-être n'est-il pas mauvais, au moment où, sous les auspices du British Council et de la *William Morris Society* de Londres, une exposition itinérante William Morris parcourt l'Europe, d'évoquer la vie ardente de cet homme tout à la fois poète, peintre, écrivain, imprimeur, tribun politique presque révolutionnaire à ses heures et compagnon d'Edouard Burne-Jones, fleuron admirable de la grande époque du préraphaélitisme.

Ce fut sans doute une jeunesse heureuse que celle de William, un parmi les neuf enfants de la famille Morris de la petite ville de Walthamstow, à l'est de

5

PLATE 80 Pamphlet on William Morris set in Bruce Rogers's Centaur type. Ornaments and intials from Morris's Kelmscott Press.

THE DISCOURSES
OF EPICTETUS

TRANSLATED BY P. E. MATHESON

ILLUSTRATED BY HANS ERNI

BERNE

PRINTED FOR THE MEMBERS OF

The Limited Editions Club

1966

PLATE 81   Title page in Garamond types for The Limited Editions Club in New York.

WOLFRAM VON DEN STEINEN

HOMO
CAELESTIS

DAS WORT DER KUNST

IM MITTELALTER

I · TEXTBAND

FRANCKE VERLAG BERN

UND MÜNCHEN

PLATE 82   Title page set entirely in Bembo capitals, meticulously letterspaced.

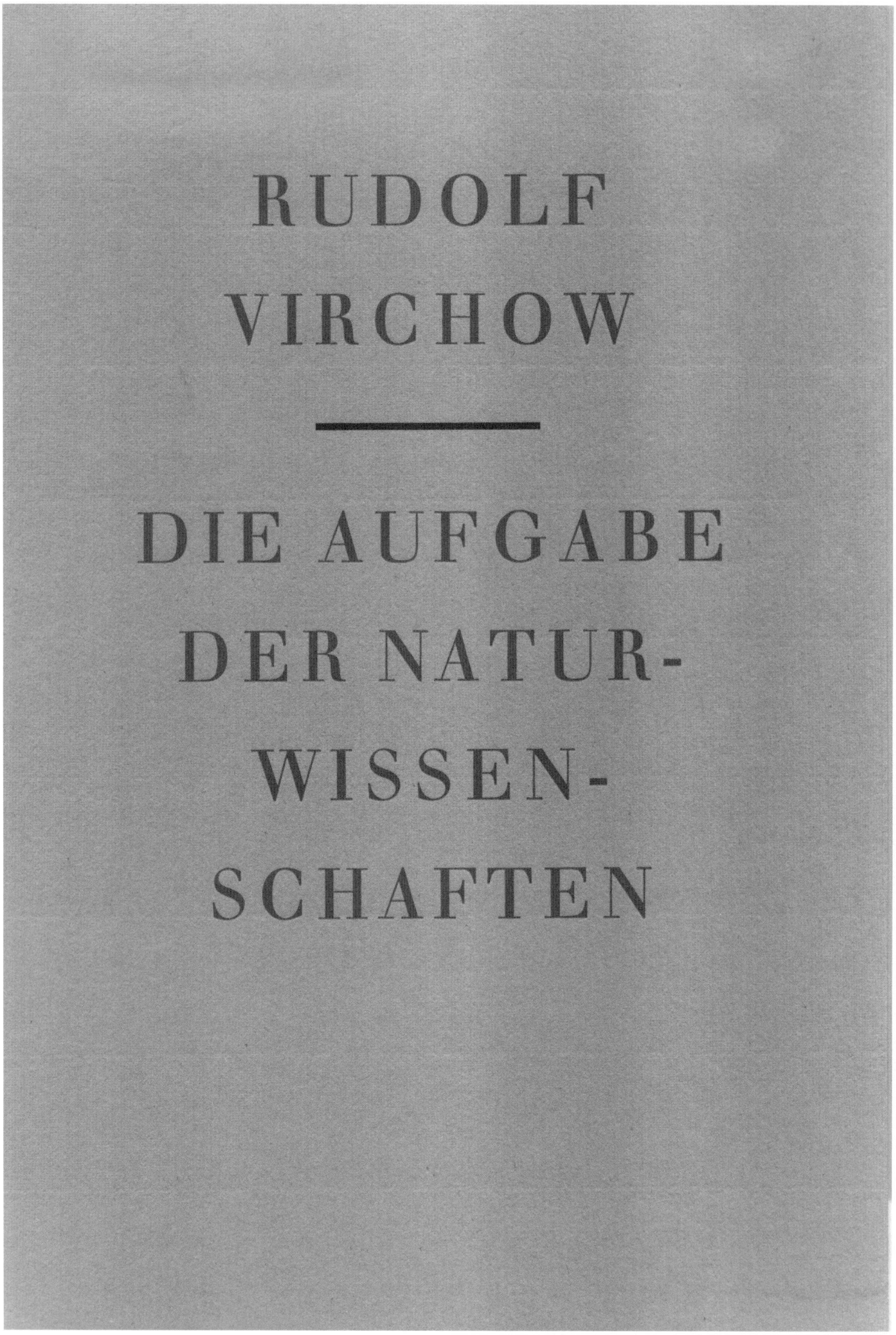

RUDOLF

VIRCHOW

———

DIE AUFGABE

DER NATUR-

WISSEN-

SCHAFTEN

PLATE 83 An attractive cover using one size only of Walbaum capitals.

Nynna L. Phenn

WACH
SEIN
IST
ALLES

Verlag Wälti Biel

PLATE 84 Sample dust jacket employing Max Caflisch's own Columna capitals (together with Weiss Italic). From the type specimen printed at the Bauer typefoundry.

Kleines Spiel

mit Ornamenten

VON MAX CAFLISCH

ANGELUS-DRUCKE

BERN

PLATE 85   Dust jacket for Caflisch's own text on the use of piece ornaments.

PASSION

BILDER VON FELIX HOFFMANN

THEOLOGISCHER VERLAG ZÜRICH

PLATE 86 A title page which is striking in its simplicity. Set in Mardersteig's Dante typeface.

Gotthard de Beauclair was one of the foremost proponents of a post-war German style that emphasizes elegance, simplicity, and close attention to detail in typography and all aspects of book production. Other proponents of this style are Richard von Sichowsky, Eugen Sporer, Gustav Stresow, and Hermann Zapf (pp. 156–171). They favor classic types (such as Bembo, Garamond, and Walbaum) or modern types in the classic vein (such as Palatino, Diotima, or Trump). They also have a traditional respect for materials – fine papers (Hahnemühle, Fabriano, Arches) and finely crafted bindings. Their type arrangements are simple but often novel, breaking out of the traditional mold. The results are functional, beautiful, and timeless volumes which are nevertheless distinctly modern.

De Beauclair was born in Ascona, Switzerland, on 24 July 1907, where he attended an Italian language school until the age of thirteen. He finished his school years in Darmstadt, Germany, where his uncle, type designer Friedrich Wilhelm Kleukens (who also ran a private press for the Duke Ernst Ludwig of Darmstadt), suggested that he study with Rudolf Koch at the Offenbach Werkstatt. During this training period he studied calligraphy with Koch, printing with the great (but unsung) typographer Ernst Engel, and composition at the Klingspor typefoundry, where he completed an apprenticeship. De Beauclair's co-students at the Werkstatt included Fritz Kredel, the famous woodcut artist, Herbert Post, designer of several types bearing his name, and Berthold Wolpe, designer of the Albertus and Pegasus types. There he also met the well-known bookbinder, Ignatz Wiemeler, and Ernst Kellner, who later became director of the Offizin Haag-Drugulin in Leipzig. Kellner persuaded de Beauclair to move to Leipzig and work in his printing shop. In Leipzig, de Beauclair again made significant acquaintances, most importantly with Anton Kippenberg who founded Insel Verlag. In 1928 Kippenberg invited de Beauclair to work for him as a book designer. Through this appointment, de Beauclair came to know Carl Ernst Poeschel, director of the printing house of Poeschel & Trepte, and Walter Tiemann, noted calligrapher and type designer. It is obvious that exposure to the great printers, calligraphers, and typographers of pre-war Germany provided fertile ground for the growth of de Beauclair's talents.

Leipzig, the pre-war center of the German book trade, was destroyed during World War II; the German publishing industry emerged from the war in a state of chaos. De Beauclair managed to escape with a single suitcase into the British zone, but he was ill and starving. His first communication from the outside world was a food parcel from his former Werkstatt classmate and fellow typographer, Henri

Friedlaender, who had suffered through the painful years of the German occupation in Holland.

After the war, de Beauclair's typographic career slowly resumed its true course. In 1951 he became a typographer and design consultant to the famous Stempel typefoundry in Frankfurt, and in the following year he also took on book design leadership at the newly formed West German branch of Insel Verlag, also in Frankfurt. During his years at Stempel, de Beauclair developed an important working relationship with Hermann Zapf and Georg Kurt Schauer. The foundry had an exceptional commitment to technical and artistic excellence; as a result, the type designs, specimens, and fine books that Stempel issued through the efforts of these men dramatically influenced the course of modern typography. The Palatino, Diotima, and Optima types, to name just a few, were extraordinary, being calligraphically based faces which were serviceable, not as idiosyncratic (and thereby restricted in usefulness) as previous German calligraphic typefaces with calligraphic origins.

De Beauclair was advisor to several type design projects. He suggested that Hermann Zapf design a type in the same family as Palatino but more suited to book work; the result was the Aldus font. He invited Jan Tschichold to develop a type based on Garamond and suitable for photocomposition, Linotype, Monotype, or for hand setting; this became Sabon.

The most important book works resulting from de Beauclair's association with Stempel are the sixteen books published under the imprint of the Trajanus Presse. The Presse was the property of Stempel with de Beauclair acting as editor, designer (with one exception: Hermann Zapf's *Feder und Stichel*), and publisher. Although he left his position at Stempel in 1959 to devote more time to Insel and other projects, he continued to work on the Trajanus Presse books until 1968. Several of these books featured the first use of a new typeface manufactured by Stempel, for example: Palatino Italic – Rilke, *Vom Alleinsein* (1951, plate 91); Balzac – *Trilussa, Die Bekehnte Schlange* (1952); Diotima – von le Fort, *Plus Ultra* (1953); and Sabon – *Der Roman von Tristan und Isolde* (1966, plate 92). The Trajanus Presse books are all extraordinary productions, and the following descriptions of three of them should serve as an indication of the qualities to be found in all sixteen.

The tenth book of the Presse was *Lucidor* by Hugo von Hofmannsthal (1959, plate 93). It is printed from Janson type cast from the original seventeenth-century matrices in the possession of the Stempel foundry, on Japanese paper folded at the fore-edges in the Japanese style. There are twelve wood engravings by Felix Hoffmann (who illustrated three other Trajanus Presse books). The typography is deceptively simple, and therefore few will notice the little details that make this such a pleasing volume. The punctuation, when occurring at the end of a line, hangs in the margin so that the line appears optically flush with the other lines of type. Similarly, capital letters such as A, T, V, and W at the beginning of a line hang in the left margin to appear aligned. The text is set justified except where type runs around a wood engraving, in which case it is set ragged. And the rose-colored ink on the title page matches the silk used to cover the boards.

Das Evangelium Johannes (1960, plate 90) is a purely typographic book. The German text is set in Aldus and the Greek – which is placed in a narrow column in the outer margins – in Heraklit. This theme of the narrow marginal column of type is repeated in the short introductory note and the colophon. Again, the simplicity of the typographic arrangement is striking and deceptive. De Beauclair's usual attention to details of composition is fully in evidence. The book is printed on a special making of Hahnemühle paper with a watermark of the Trajanus Presse logo. On those leaves in which the watermark appears, it aligns with the narrow column of Greek text. The book is bound by Willy Pingel in full leather with a blind-embossed cross pattern.

The fifteenth publication, *Der Roman von Tristan und Isolde* (1966, plate 92), is again an illustrated book. Fritz Kredel executed woodcuts (hand-colored) in a pseudo-renaissance style, yet with a modern flavor. The type is Jan Tschichold's Sabon roman, with display set in an ancient Schwabacher type, cast at Stempel from the original matrices. The 112 pages were hand set by Walter Wilkes, who later went on to do exceptional work at the Technische Hochschule in Darmstadt.

In addition to the Trajanus Presse books, de Beauclair produced fine editions under two other imprints: Ars Librorum and Edition de Beauclair. The Ars Librorum books are illustrated in the tradition of the French *livres d'artiste*, but without the overemphasis on the pictures to the detriment of the text evident in many French publications. Here, text and illustration are each beautiful in their own right, and both work together harmoniously. The craftsmanship, materials, and even the general overall aesthetic of these editions are not dissimilar to those of the Trajanus Presse, but Verlag Ars Librorum was de Beauclair's own independent imprint: therefore, he could have the freedom to use a wider range of typefaces and content than at the Trajanus Presse, which was part of the Stempel typefoundry. The second Ars Librorum title, *Das unschätzbare Schloss in der afrikanischen Höhle Xa Xa*, exhibits the principles of fine materials, perfect execution, and a modern yet classical typography while using Walbaum type – a font not available at Stempel, yet one with sharp edges and a somewhat strong color that harmonizes perfectly with the illustrations by Wilfried Blecher. Walbaum was also employed by de Beauclair for an Insel Verlag compilation of Haiku poetry (plate 95). There was some overlap of these two imprints: the Trajanus Presse was active from 1951 through 1972; the first Ars Librorum title appeared in 1962.

In 1966, the first Edition de Beauclair was published. These large-format publications provided a forum for the visual artist; the illustrations are the focus and the text is secondary. The thirteen titles contain lithographs, etchings, or drypoints by such noted artists as Max Peiffer-Watenphul, Giorgio de Chirico, and Jean Moréas. There is a remarkable duality in de Beauclair's work. Using the most precious materials and the finest craft techniques, he produced limited edition books that rival the finest exemplars of the art of bookmaking, yet he did not shun the production of large commercial editions. Indeed, through his work for Insel, Propyläen, and other commercial publishers, de Beauclair showed that with care, an ordinary edition can be finely done. As a lover of beautiful books and not merely a devotee of fine materials, he aimed to create exceptional books within the limitations presented to him. His work shows that the most important factor in book manufacture is the intelligent and tasteful handling of typography, materials, and processes. How could one improve, for example, on his design for the dust jacket of an Insel Verlag edition of Rilke poetry (plate 89)? Even though inexpensive, the Insel volumes (plates 87–89) show care in the minutest details; the board bindings are sometimes elegantly stamped with calligraphic designs, or often have pasted labels on front and spine. Admittedly, few readers appreciate the intricacies of bookmaking, as de Beauclair is well aware, writing:

As music needs the well trained listener, typography assumes a corresponding ability of the reader to view books in such a way that the shape of the letter and the page, and the general design of the volume, appear not as something incidental and interchangeable but as an optical realization of the words.

The work of de Beauclair stands as a model of fine bookmaking over a broad range of budgets and manufacturing techniques. Of course, credit must be given to the publishers who encouraged his work and were willing to spend slightly more to allow this to be accomplished. There was a time when trade publishers in Germany, such as Insel and Propyläen, would occasionally go to the extra expense of special features such as mould-made paper, a second color on the title page, and fine binding – all of which are incorporated in the sumptuous editions of *Das Bamberger Apokalypse* designed by de Beauclair for Insel, and the *Die Darmstädter Pessach-Haggadah* for Propyläen. More recently trade book manufacture has sadly declined – even in Germany where tasteful design and above-average production quality were the rule, rather than the exception, well into the late 1960s. The fine printing being done by private presses today in small pockets on both sides of the Atlantic is often pretentious and almost always prohibitively expensive. We can rejoice in the work of many great book artists active in producing both trade and fine publications in the twentieth century. It seems the possibilities for working simultaneously on the production of beautiful books in both large commercial runs and fine limited editions have become quite slim. I fear that de Beauclair may have been correct in writing as early as 1966: "An earlier generation of publishers who with shrewd perception worked in close collaboration with an active group of designers has ceased to exist." When he died on 31 March 1992 the situation had not gotten any better.

*

In 1951 Gotthard de Beauclair was appointed art director of the Stempel Typefoundry in Frankfurt, Germany. It was a title he shared with Hermann Zapf, who was more than ten years younger. Both men espoused a similar approach to book design, though Zapf's work is much better known through his type designs. Zapf's Palatino Italic font was first used in a book designed by de Beauclair for his Trajanus Presse imprint, and his seminal calligraphic manual, *Feder und Stichel* (*Pen and Graver* in English), was published at de Beauclair's Trajanus Presse (the only book published under that imprint which was not designed by de Beauclair himself). Many of de Beauclair's finest editions were set in Zapf typefaces (*Das Buch Joram* and *Amor & Psyche* (plate 94) in Palatino, *Das Evangelium Johannes* in Aldus and Heraklit, the translation of the *Psalms* in Aldus italic, etc.). There were also ties through the Insel publishing house, where de Beauclair served as art director, in which capacity he commissioned Zapf to do many binding lettering pieces, and even the entire Greek text of one book by hand (the 1951 Insel edition of the writings of Heraclitus, which would form the basis for Zapf's first Greek typeface, appropriately christened "Heraklit").

LUDWIG AURBACHER

Die Abenteuer von den sieben Schwaben

MIT ZEICHNUNGEN VON

PETER HOFFER

ERSCHIENEN IM INSEL-VERLAG

PLATE 87 Title page from one of the books published by Insel Bücherei. Gotthard de Beauclair designed hundreds of books for this series.

146

Deutsche Holzschnitte
des
XX. Jahrhunderts

Insel-Bücherei Nr. 606

PLATE 88 Decorated paper cover for one of the Insel Bücherei series.

*Rainer
Maria Rilke*

—

*Duineser
Elegien*

IM INSEL-VERLAG

PLATE 89 A dust jacket for Insel Verlag set in Garamond italic.

sandt hast. ²⁶Und ich habe ihnen deinen Namen kundgetan und will ihn kundtun, damit die Liebe, mit der du mich liebst, sei in ihnen und ich in ihnen.

18 Da Jesus solches geredet hatte, ging er hinaus mit seinen Jüngern über den Bach Kidron; da war ein Garten, darein ging Jesus und seine Jünger. ²Judas aber, der ihn verriet, wußte den Ort auch, denn Jesus versammelte sich oft daselbst mit seinen Jüngern. ³Da nun Judas zu sich genommen hatte die Schar der Kriegsknechte und die Diener der Hohenpriester und Pharisäer, kommt er dahin mit Fackeln, Lampen und mit Waffen. ⁴Da nun Jesus wußte alles, was ihm begegnen sollte, ging er hinaus und sprach zu ihnen: Wen suchet ihr? ⁵Sie antworteten ihm: Jesus von Nazareth. Er spricht zu ihnen: Ich bin's! Judas aber, der ihn verriet, stand auch bei ihnen. ⁶Als nun Jesus zu ihnen sprach: Ich bin's! wichen sie zurück und fielen zu Boden. ⁷Da fragte er sie abermals: Wen suchet ihr? Sie aber sprachen: Jesus von Nazareth. ⁸Jesus antwortete: Ich habe es euch gesagt, daß ich's bin. Suchet ihr denn mich, so lasset diese gehen! ⁹auf daß das Wort erfüllt würde, welches er gesagt hatte: Ich habe derer keinen verloren, die du mir gegeben hast. ¹⁰Da hatte Simon Petrus ein Schwert und zog es heraus und schlug nach des Hohenpriesters Knecht und hieb ihm sein rechtes Ohr ab. Und der Knecht hieß Malchus. ¹¹Da sprach Jesus zu Petrus: Stecke dein Schwert in die Scheide! Soll ich den Kelch nicht trinken, den mir mein Vater gegeben hat?

¹²Die Schar aber und der Oberhauptmann und die Diener der Juden nahmen Jesus und banden ihn ¹³und führten ihn zuerst zu Hannas; der war der Schwiegervater des Kaiphas, welcher des Jahres Hoherpriester war. ¹⁴Es war aber Kaiphas, der den Juden geraten hatte, es wäre gut, daß EIN Mensch stürbe für das Volk.

¹⁵Simon Petrus aber folgte Jesus nach und ein anderer Jünger. Dieser Jünger war dem Hohenpriester bekannt und ging mit Jesus hinein in des Hohenpriesters Palast. ¹⁶Petrus aber stand draußen vor der Tür. Da ging der andere Jünger, der dem Hohenpriester bekannt war, hinaus und redete mit der Türhüterin und führte Petrus hinein. ¹⁷Da sprach die Magd, die Türhüterin, zu Petrus: Bist du nicht auch einer von den Jüngern dieses Menschen? Er sprach: Ich bin's nicht. ¹⁸Es standen aber die

τοι ἔγνωσαν ὅτι σύ με ἀπέστειλας· καὶ ἐγνώρισα αὐτοῖς τὸ ὄνομά σου καὶ γνωρίσω, ἵνα ἡ ἀγάπη ἣν ἠγάπησάς με ἐν αὐτοῖς ᾖ κἀγὼ ἐν αὐτοῖς.

Ταῦτα εἰπὼν Ἰησοῦς ἐξῆλθεν σὺν τοῖς μαθηταῖς αὐτοῦ πέραν τοῦ χειμάρρου τοῦ Κεδρών, ὅπου ἦν κῆπος, εἰς ὃν εἰσῆλθεν αὐτὸς καὶ οἱ μαθηταὶ αὐτοῦ. ᾔδει δὲ καὶ Ἰούδας ὁ παραδιδοὺς αὐτὸν τὸν τόπον, ὅτι πολλάκις συνήχθη Ἰησοῦς ἐκεῖ μετὰ τῶν μαθητῶν αὐτοῦ. ὁ οὖν Ἰούδας λαβὼν τὴν σπεῖραν καὶ ἐκ τῶν ἀρχιερέων καὶ ἐκ τῶν Φαρισαίων ὑπηρέτας ἔρχεται ἐκεῖ μετὰ φανῶν καὶ λαμπάδων καὶ ὅπλων. Ἰησοῦς οὖν εἰδὼς πάντα τὰ ἐρχόμενα ἐπ' αὐτὸν ἐξῆλθεν καὶ λέγει αὐτοῖς· τίνα ζητεῖτε; ἀπεκρίθησαν αὐτῷ· Ἰησοῦν τὸν Ναζωραῖον. λέγει αὐτοῖς· ἐγώ εἰμι. εἱστήκει δὲ καὶ Ἰούδας ὁ παραδιδοὺς αὐτὸν μετ' αὐτῶν. ὡς οὖν εἶπεν αὐτοῖς· ἐγώ εἰμι, ἀπῆλθαν εἰς τὰ ὀπίσω καὶ ἔπεσαν χαμαί. πάλιν οὖν ἐπηρώτησεν αὐτούς· τίνα ζητεῖτε; οἱ δὲ εἶπαν· Ἰησοῦν τὸν Ναζωραῖον. ἀπεκρίθη Ἰησοῦς· εἶπον ὑμῖν ὅτι ἐγώ εἰμι· εἰ οὖν ἐμὲ ζητεῖτε, ἄφετε τούτους ὑπάγειν· ἵνα πληρωθῇ ὁ λόγος ὃν εἶπεν, ὅτι οὓς δέδωκάς μοι, οὐκ ἀπώλεσα ἐξ αὐτῶν οὐδένα. Σίμων οὖν Πέτρος ἔχων μάχαιραν εἵλκυσεν αὐτὴν καὶ ἔπαισεν τὸν τοῦ ἀρχιερέως δοῦλον καὶ ἀπέκοψεν αὐτοῦ τὸ ὠτάριον τὸ δεξιόν· ἦν δὲ ὄνομα τῷ δούλῳ Μάλχος. εἶπεν οὖν ὁ Ἰησοῦς τῷ Πέτρῳ· βάλε τὴν μάχαιραν εἰς τὴν θήκην· τὸ ποτήριον ὃ δέδωκέν μοι ὁ πατήρ, οὐ μὴ πίω αὐτό;

Ἡ οὖν σπεῖρα καὶ ὁ χιλίαρχος καὶ οἱ ὑπηρέται τῶν Ἰουδαίων συνέλαβον τὸν Ἰησοῦν καὶ ἔδησαν αὐτόν, καὶ ἤγαγον πρὸς Ἄνναν πρῶτον· ἦν γὰρ πενθερὸς τοῦ Καϊάφα, ὃς ἦν ἀρχιερεὺς τοῦ ἐνιαυτοῦ ἐκείνου· ἦν δὲ Καϊάφας ὁ συμβουλεύσας τοῖς Ἰουδαίοις ὅτι συμφέρει ἕνα ἄνθρωπον ἀποθανεῖν ὑπὲρ τοῦ λαοῦ. Ἠκολούθει δὲ τῷ Ἰησοῦ Σίμων Πέτρος καὶ ἄλλος μαθητής. ὁ δὲ μαθητὴς ἐκεῖνος ἦν γνωστὸς τῷ ἀρχιερεῖ, καὶ συνεισῆλθεν τῷ Ἰησοῦ εἰς τὴν αὐλὴν τοῦ ἀρχιερέως, ὁ δὲ Πέτρος εἱστήκει πρὸς τῇ θύρᾳ ἔξω. ἐξῆλθεν οὖν ὁ μαθητὴς ὁ ἄλλος ὁ γνωστὸς τοῦ ἀρχιερέως καὶ εἶπεν τῇ θυρωρῷ, καὶ εἰσήγαγεν τὸν Πέτρον. λέγει οὖν τῷ Πέτρῳ ἡ παιδίσκη ἡ θυρωρός· μὴ καὶ σὺ ἐκ τῶν μαθητῶν εἶ τοῦ ἀνθρώπου τούτου;

43

PLATE 90 Text page from *Das Evangelium Johannes* (Frankfurt, Trajanus Presse, 1960) in Hermann Zapf's Aldus and Heraklit types, with verse number in Zapf's Michelangelo Titling – all Stempel typefaces.

München, am Allerheiligentage 1915

*Es ist mir, Herr Jomar Förste, wie ein Vorwurf, zu
sehen, daß Ihr guter Brief, den ich wieder las, das
Datum des 28ten August trägt. Hab ich so lange
nicht geantwortet?*

*Das ist das einzige Gute dieser ins unverantwort-
lichste Geschehn verpflichteten Wochen, Monate,
daß sie rascher als andere hinzustürzen scheinen, als
wünschten sie selber nichts, wie vorbei zu sein und
fürchteten, man könne sie fragen, wohin sie's treiben.
Wenigstens mir hier entgeht Zeit um Zeit, die Un-
wirklichkeit, die das alles für mich hat, trägt wohl
dazu bei, es dahinzuwirbeln: Denn wo wäre ein
Tag, den man faßte, sich zu eigen machte, im genauen
geistigen Sinne? Es sind nur unfaßliche da.*

*Das Abseits-Sein, von dem Sie in Ihrem Briefe
erzählen, ist mir, der ich nie eine andere Einrichtung
gekannt habe, nichts Verwunderliches. Wie nun*

PLATE 91   From *Vom Alleinsein* (Trajanus Presse), the first book set in Hermann Zapf's Palatino Italic font.

150

Der Roman von Tristan und Isolde

ERNEUT VON JOSEPH BEDIER / IN DER ÜBERTRAGUNG

RUDOLF G. BINDINGS / MIT VIERZEHN HOLZSCHNITTEN

VON FRITZ KREDEL / EINE LIEBHABERAUSGABE DER

TRAJANUS-PRESSE ZU FRANKFURT AM MAIN

PLATE 92 Title page in Tschichold's Sabon type (its first use) with hand-colored woodcuts by Fritz Kredel.

Arabella, die mit ziemlich erho-
benen Stimmen im sonderbar-
sten Dialog begriffen sind.

Wladimir hat am Vormittag
Arabellas geheimnisvollen Ab-
schiedsbrief empfangen. Nie
hat etwas sein Herz so getrof-
fen. Er fühlt, daß zwischen ihm
und ihr etwas Dunkles stehe,
aber nicht zwischen Herz und
Herz. Er fühlt die Liebe und
die Kraft in sich, es zu erfahren,
zu begreifen, zu verzeihen, sei
es, was es sei. Er hat die unver-
gleichliche Geliebte seiner
Nächte zu lieb, um ohne sie zu
leben. Seltsamerweise denkt er
gar nicht an die wirkliche Arabella, fast kommt es ihm son-

36

PLATE 93   Text spread from the Trajanus Presse edition of *Lucidor* (1956) set in Janson.
Woodcuts by Felix Hoffmann.

lerbar vor, daß sie es sein wird, der er gegenüberzutreten
hat, um sie zu beschwichtigen, aufzurichten, sie ganz und
für immer zu gewinnen. Er kommt hin, findet im Salon die
Mutter allein. Sie ist aufgeregt, wirr und phantastisch wie
nur je. Er ist anders, als sie ihn je gesehen hat. Er küßt ihr
die Hände, er spricht, alles in einer gerührten, befangenen
Weise. Er bittet sie, ihm ein Gespräch unter vier Augen
mit Arabella zu gestatten. Frau von Murska ist entzückt und
ohne Übergang in allen Himmeln. Das Unwahrscheinliche
ist ihr Element. Sie eilt, Arabella zu holen, dringt in sie, dem
edlen jungen Mann nun, wo alles sich so herrlich gewendet,
ihr Ja nicht zu versagen. Arabella ist maßlos erstaunt. ›Ich
gehe durchaus nicht so mit ihm‹, sagt sie kühl. ›Man ahnt
nie, wie man mit Männern steht‹, entgegnet ihr die Mutter
und schickt sie in den Salon. Wladimir ist verlegen, er-
griffen und glühend. Arabella findet mehr und mehr, daß Herr
von Imfanger recht habe, Wladimir einen sonderbaren
Herrn zu finden. Wladimir, durch ihre Kühle aus der Fassung,
bittet sie, nun endlich die Maske fallen zu lassen. Arabella

37

APULEJUS

AMOR UND PSYCHE

MIT SECHS RADIERUNGEN

VON FELIX HOFFMANN

ERSCHIENEN

IM VERLAG ARS LIBRORUM

GOTTHARD DE BEAUCLAIR

FRANKFURT AM MAIN

MCMLXIII

PLATE 94   Title page of a volume published by de Beauclair's Verlag Ars Librorum.

HAIKU *Japanische Dreizeiler*

AUSGEWÄHLT UND AUS DEM URTEXT

ÜBERTRAGEN VON JAN ULENBROOK

IM INSEL-VERLAG · MCMLX

PLATE 95   Exemplary design in Walbaum types for an inexpensive trade edition.

HERMANN ZAPF

Hermann Zapf is justly famous among typographers for his type designs. Palatino (1949), Melior (1952), and the revolutionary Optima (1958), are three of the most popular typefaces available today. Amazingly, the modern-looking Palatino roman and its companion italic were released almost a half-century ago, when Zapf, who was born on 8 November 1918, was a mere 31 years old. His newer alphabets for ITC (Zapf International, Zapf Chancery), Linotype (Zapfino), and others also enjoy wide use. Of the ten types resident on every Macintosh computer when shipped, four – Palatino, Optima, Zapf Chancery, and Zapf Dingbats, were designed by Hermann Zapf.

Zapf is equally famous in the world of calligraphy, where his work was first brought to the attention of those in the United States interested in that subject through an exhibition organized by Paul Standard in 1951 at The Cooper Union in New York. The exhibition displayed work by Zapf as well as Fritz Kredel, the great illustrator and woodcut artist who studied with Rudolf Koch in Offenbach, Germany.

In addition, collectors of typography and fine printing will also be familiar with the magnificent *Manuale Typographicum* I (1954) and II (1968), each with 100 typographical arrangements by Zapf, and *Typographic Variations* (1963), which displays seventy-eight of his designs for text and title-pages. However, we will not elaborate further on these contributions to the letter arts here, but instead consider a lesser-known aspect of Zapf's work – his book design.

Most people associate Zapf's typography only with the new and experimental *Manuale Typographicum,* which displays beautiful arrangements of a wide variety of typefaces in many languages. This is misleading because most of the playful arrangements of that work are not addressed to the practical needs of books, as Zapf himself is well aware. For example, almost never would he set text running vertically on the page, use violently contrasting type sizes, or disturb a running text in order to create a typographic effect – yet all these devices occur in the *Manuale.* Regrettably, these devices are seen all too frequently in contemporary book design. Zapf's own book design, however, displays his understanding that the purpose of books is, as Thomas James Cobden-Sanderson wrote, "to communicate to the imagination, without loss by the way, the thought or image intended to be communicated by the author."

Zapf's basic philosophy of book design rests first and foremost on the premise that the book is a functional object. While his work is often innovative and sometimes playful, it is not radically removed from the concept of the book as a vessel for information. He is therefore respectful of the traditions of sound book typography, which, as he has stated, still allow the fertile mind much room for creativity. He writes:

Many designers apparently hesitate to use the true but "old" proportions to avoid being considered old-fashioned. But a book that is meant to be read should comply with certain functions. . . . There are enough other possibilities and ways to prove one's art and skill, even if a designer feels he should express his ideas in a very eye-catching way.

Zapf agrees with Daniel Berkeley Updike (pp. 4–17) that a book must reflect "the taste or feeling of its time." He seldom uses old-fashioned ornamentation, and when he does it is employed only sparingly, in a more modern, less fancy way. As he wrote in 1966, "our objective should be a typography aimed at legibility and clarity, self-evident in disposition, free from unnecessary 'extras' or ornaments." He avoids any tricks with running heads, folios, or chapter openings. He does not practice allusive typography. Many important typographers covered earlier in this book, such as Bruce Rogers, D. B. Updike, and Francis Meynell, based their book designs on this working method, and indeed few would deny that they created beautiful books through this practice. However, Zapf has said, "it would be an anachronism if a book by a contemporary author, who deals with the problems of our time . . . were designed in the style of the 16th or 17th centuries." Rather, his typography relies on the delicate placement and careful manipulation of type, space, publisher's device, and occasionally calligraphy or illustration. Elegant proportions (often based on the classic golden section) and a sensitive handling of the various elements are paramount in Zapf's design. In this regard, his work is similar to that of Jan van Krimpen or Jan Tschichold, but without the rigid division between the asymmetrical and the classical styles of the latter, and with more boldness and innovation than the former. One might draw an analogy between Zapf's book design and Chinese painting, both relying greatly on the tension between space and a few simple elements for effect. Zapf's restrained use of beautiful type and appropriate materials – with minimal decoration or reliance on older styles of book design – reflects a significant break with the fine book design of the era immediately preceding him.

In keeping with his philosophy of the modern book, Zapf favors contemporary types over recuttings of historic designs, and he does not avoid modern book production methods. We see much more of the modern typefaces Aldus and Trump in Zapf's books than recuttings of historical fonts such as Bembo or Bell – yet he has used all these types at some time.

Much of the fine printing done earlier in this century relied on handmade paper and handset type, often printed on a hand press. Zapf has, however, embraced the newer technologies – from Linotype to digital composition, and from machine letterpress through offset and even xerography – to produce books of lasting quality and great beauty. Printing itself is a machine technology which supplanted calligraphy for general use, and from it came a wholly new art, to be used in different ways and for different purposes than its predecessor. In some ways printing surpassed calligraphy, in others it never equalled it, but it has its own ethos.

Many of Zapf's designs could be considered classical in arrangement – see, for example, Virgil's *Bucolica* (plate 98) or the elegant *Divina Proportio Typographica*, or Zapf's first work as author, *William Morris: His Work and Life*. These few examples show how Zapf uses the customary components of symmetrical arrangement, careful spacing and choice of type styles and sizes to create a most pleasing volume. The result is very close to the later work of Jan Tschichold, and something similar is often found in that of Giovanni Mardersteig. The latter was fully cognizant of Zapf's achievement in book design, observing in his talk delivered upon the occasion of the award of the Gutenberg Prize to Zapf in 1974, "It has often been a pleasure for me to take in hand a book that Hermann Zapf has thought through typographically." Mardersteig had, by the way, won this prestigious prize several years earlier, in 1968. This relationship between two of this century's greatest, if very different, typographers is not well known and scarcely documented.

As well as his work in traditional style, Zapf has produced some of the most innovative book design of the last half of the twentieth century, and has accomplished this without allowing his books to become a vehicle for the typographer's ego rather than the author's ideas. So much contemporary "fine printing" seems to suffer from just this fault. Zapf is creative without being obtrusive, as will be immediately evident from looking at some of his work. For example, a novel use of the half-title and title-page is shown in Walter Riezler's *Beethoven*. Here the information which traditionally appears on the title page (author, title, publisher, place, etc.) is placed on the half-title; only the author's name and a facsimile of Beethoven's signature are on the title. The resulting layout is extraordinarily dramatic, with the sparse title page facing a full-bleed portrait of Beethoven.

Zapf also likes to use the double-page title spread, with ingenious variations. Examples of this are *Wunderlichstes Buch der Bücher* (1960), several books of the work of Nelly Sachs designed for Suhrkamp in the sixties, and *Don Quixote* (1969). In the first-named, the title is on the verso in red, with the subtitle and author on the recto in black. In the Nelly Sachs books the publisher's name is on the verso, with author, title, and blind-embossed publisher's mark on the recto. In *Don Quixote* the title and subtitle are on the recto, and author, publisher, and translator are on the verso.

Zapf rarely uses more than three or four type sizes for any one book, and occasionally, he employs only one size throughout. In this he agrees with Tschichold that "it is a good rule to restrict the number of typefaces used . . . as much as possible; three sizes are often sufficient." The Zapf Typophile Chapbook, *About Alphabets* (1960, plate 96), employs essentially just one size and style of type. The two kinds of text (main text and commentary), captions, headings, folios, colophon, etc. are all set in 10-point Optima, but by the ingenious use of leading and careful placement, with some lines of letterspaced capitals, he has made this one size work clearly and harmoniously for very different kinds of matter. On title pages, also, Zapf sometimes restricts himself to one size and style of type. Examples are the Bible in Greek and German for *Liber Librorum* (1955), and Oskar Loerke's *Gedichte und Prosa* (1958). Other title pages of his rely on traditional elements for their effect.

Among Zapf's more traditional designs is the notable series of charming little books on German cities which he designed for Hermann Emig in Amorbach (plate 99). The series is uniform in format and profusely illustrated, usually with color and folding plates, as well as halftones. These books show great care in the small details of bookmaking, and they benefit from the collaboration of two fine craftsmen who have done much to maintain the high quality of German books: printer Ludwig Oehms, and binder Willy Pingel. Oehms was a compositor at Stempel when Zapf was art director there; he later began his own typesetting and printing plant. There he printed *About Alphabets* (except for the type specimens which were printed at Stempel), and the second *Manuale Typographicum*. Pingel bound *About Alphabets* and *Typographic Variations*, and many other volumes for Zapf (and also for Gotthard de Beauclair). Several of the Emig books, like so many of Zapf's designs, are enlivened by his superb calligraphy. He displays a complete mastery of this ancient art as well as faultless taste in its application to book work, whether it be blackletter (*Kranichstein* and *Bekenntnisse zur Humanität*), uncial (*Zucht und Schöne Sitte*), italic (*Balthasar Neumann*), or roman capitals (*International Letterhead Review* and *Amyntas*, plate 102). Often his calligraphy is used on a binding (*Leben beginnt mit Liebe* and quite a few trade volumes designed by Gotthard de Beauclair for the Insel publishing house), and occasionally he has drawn special initials, as in *Des Kaisers neue Kleider*, which was the first use of his fraktur type, Gilgengart. Occasionally Zapf has created a book in which the text is almost entirely in calligraphy, such as the Greek text for the Insel edition of the works of Heraclitus.

Zapf has designed books for composition on every kind of typesetting system from handset foundry type to Linotype and Monotype, photocomposition and digital character generation. The faces he uses most often are his own designs, Aldus and Optima, and the Diotima of his wife, Gudrun. He also uses Trump Mediaeval and some of the older classic faces such as Bembo, Garamond, Baskerville, and Walbaum repeatedly. It is interesting that he uses Aldus much more frequently than the related Palatino, the former being a lighter type with slightly more conventional letterforms, better suited to books than is the heavier Palatino. One book in which he did use Palatino is *Deutsche Buchdrucker des Fünfzehnten Jahrhunderts* for Otto Harrassowitz. Here the slightly heavier Palatino on the verso text pages helps to balance the illustrations of blackletter or semi-gothic types on the rectos. Optima he uses sparingly, mainly for catalogues and texts of a more scientific turn, such as Rosarivo's *Divina Proportio Typographica*. Gudrun Zapf von Hesse's Diotima has not been available for hot-metal machine composition and therefore Zapf could use it only for special editions such as Nelly Sachs's *Die Suchende*, or Tasso's *Amyntas* (plate 102), this latter with aquatint etchings printed by Mardersteig.

*

Hermann Zapf's most important contribution to the field of book design is the production of volumes which are contemporary but imbued with a classic taste and elegance. At the beginning of the twentieth-century, masters of book design borrowed elements from books of the past and made them their own. In the twenties and thirties, some typographers revolted against what they considered such anachronism, and developed a so-called "modern" typography. Generally they went too far, and much of their work is bleak and sterile. In the modern age of rapid technological change and constant transition in production methods, Zapf shows us that we need not fight or deplore such changes. Rather, we should (and can) manipulate the apparatus at our disposal, using the machines to their and our best advantage. It is feasible, his design tells us, to produce books which are of our time, but which are eternal in their beauty and quality.

ABOUT Alphabets·

SOME MARGINAL NOTES ON

TYPE DESIGN

by HERMANN Zapf

THE TYPOPHILES · NEW YORK

MCMLX

PLATE 96 Title page in Optima for Zapf's autobiographical chapbook,
published by The Typophiles of New York City.

Typographic Variations

With prefaces written by Paul Standard, New York,

designed by Hermann Zapf

G. K. Schauer, Frankfurt, and Charles Peignot, Paris,

on themes in contemporary

together with commentary notes and specifications.

book design and typography

Published 1964 by Museum Books, New York

in 78 book- and title-pages

PLATE 97   An entirely different title page in Optima for a selection of book pages designed by Zapf.

PLATE 98

Text spread from a
bilingual edition of
Virgil's *Bucolica*.
Frankfurt: Suhrkamp
Verlag, 1957. Printed
from Diotima type.
The woodcut
illustrations by
Maillol are
reproduced from the
Cranach Presse
edition of 1926.

ECLOGA SECUNDA

ALEXIS

Formosum pastor Corydon ardebat Alexim,
delicias domini; nec quid speraret habebat.
tantum inter densas umbrosa cacumina fagos
adsidue veniebat. ibi haec incondita solus
montibus et silvis studio iactabat inani:
O crudelis Alexi nihil mea carmina curas?
nil nostri miserere? mori me denique coges.

14

ZWEITES GEDICHT

ALEXIS

Corydon brannte, der Hirt, für den reizenden Knaben Alexis;
Den aber liebte sein Herr: so war ihm keinerlei Hoffnung.
Nur unterm schattigen Dach der dichtverschlungenen Buchen
Fand er sich täglich ein und sang vergebenen Trachtens
Wäldern und Bergen umher die kunstlos rührende Klage:

»Grausamer, sag, Alexis, so gilt mein Singen dir gar nichts?
Rührt mein Leiden dich nicht? Du zwingst mich, wahrlich, zu sterben
Selber das Vieh sucht jetzt die Kühlung unter den Schatten,
Selbst die grüne Lazerte verbirgt sich unter den Dornen.
Über den Mittag ruhn die ermatteten Schnitter, indessen
Thestylis Quendel und Knoblauch mischt, die riechende Mahlzeit.
Aber mit meinem Gesang, der Alexis' lieblicher Spur folgt,
Schrillt unterm glühenden Tag der Hain von lauten Zikaden.
War's nicht übergenug, Amaryllidis widriges Zürnen
Und verletzenden Stolz und den bösen Menalcas zu dulden?
Schwarz war jener gewiß; und du bist golden: o Schöner,
Trau der Farbe nicht allzusehr! Man läßt ja des Weißdorns
Blüte verwehen und pflückt Hyazinthen, ob sie auch schwarz sind.
Du aber siehst mich gar nicht an, noch weißt du, Alexis,
Wer ich sei, wie reich ich an wolligen Schafen und Milch sei:
Tausend weiden für mich am Hang sizilischer Berge;
Nie fehlt mir frischmolkene Milch, nicht sommers noch winters;
Traun, und ich singe, wie einst der thebanische Sänger Amphion
Am Aracynthus sang und rief die schweifenden Rinder.
Bin ich doch gar so häßlich nicht: ich sahe mich jüngst erst,
Als am Gestade das Meer ganz windstill ruhte. Nicht Daphnis
Fürcht ich — richte du selbst —, dafern der Spiegel nicht falsch war.

15

GISELA SIEBERT

Kranichſtein

JAGDSCHLOSS DER LANDGRAFEN

VON HESSEN-DARMSTADT

Was gleicht wohl auf Erden
dem Jägervergnügen?
Wem ſprudelt der Becher des Lebens
ſo reich?
Beim Klange der Hörner
im Grünen zu liegen,
den Hirſch zu verfolgen durch Dickicht
und Teich!

Erschienen bei Hermann Emig

Buchhändler in Amorbach

PLATE 99 One of a series of books on German localities designed
by Zapf and published by Hermann Emig. "Kranichstein" is hand-
lettered.

Johann Sebastian Bach
1685 – 1750

Messe in h-moll

BWV 232

Missa
Symbolum Nicenum
Sanctus
Osanna · Benedictus · Agnes Dei
et Dona nobis
pacem

Studienpartitur

PLATE 100 Title page design for a music score from *Typographic Variations*. New York: Museum Books, 1963. Zapf's classical side, with hand-lettered title line.

CAPUT I

1 IN PRINCIPIO ERAT
VERBUM&VERBUM
ERAT APUD DEUM/
& DEUS ERAT VER-
2 BUM · HOC ERAT
IN PRINCIPIO APUD
3 DEUM · OMNIA
PER IPSUM FACTA
SUNT & SINE IPSO
FACTUM EST NIHIL/
QUOD FACTUM
4 EST/ IN IPSO VITA
ERAT & VITA ERAT
LUX HOMINUM ·
5 & LUX IN TENEBRIS
LUCET/ & TENEBRÆ
EAM NON COM-
PREHENDERUNT ·

Fuit homo missus a Deo, cui nomen 6
erat Joannes. Hic venit in testimo- 7
nium, ut testimonium perhiberet de
lumine, ut omnes crederent per illum.
Non erat ille lux, sed ut testimonium 8
perhiberet de lumine. Erat lux vera, 9
quæ illuminat omnem hominem ve-
nientem in hunc mundum. In mun- 10
do erat, et mundus per ipsum factus
est, et mundus eum non cognovit. In 11
propria venit, et sui eum non receperunt. Quotquot autem receperunt 12
eum, dedit eis potestatem filios Dei
fieri, his, qui credunt in nomine ejus:
Qui non ex sanguinibus, neque ex 13
voluntate carnis, neque ex voluntate
viri, sed ex Deo nati sunt. Et Verbum 14
caro factum est, et habitavit in nobis: et vidimus gloriam ejus, gloriam
quasi Unigeniti a Patre plenum gra-
tiæ et veritatis. Joannes testimonium 15
perhibet de ipso, et clamat dicens:
Hic erat, quem dixi: Qui post me ven-
turus est, ante me factus est: quia prior
me erat. Et de plenitudine ejus nos om- 16
nes accepimus, et gratiam pro gratia.
Quia lex per Moysen data est, gratia, 17
et veritas per Jesum Christum facta
est. Deum nemo vidit umquam: unige- 18
nitus Filius, qui est in sinu Patris, ipse
enarravit. Et hoc est testimonium Jo- 19
annis, quando miserunt Judæi ab Je-
rosolymis sacerdotes et Levitas ad
eum ut interrogarent eum: Tu quis es?
Et confessus est, et non negavit: et con- 20
fessus est: Quia non sum ego Christus.
Et interrogaverunt eum: Quid ergo? 21
Elias es tu? Et dixit: Non sum. Pro-
pheta es tu? Et respondit: Non. —

21

PLATE 101 Text page design for a Bible from a Palatino type specimen book.

TORQUATO TASSO

AMYNTAS

Ein Schäferspiel

Aus dem Italienischen übertragen

von Hanns Studniczka

Mit acht Radierungen von

Bruno Cassinari

Erschienen bei Carl Hanser

im Jahre 1966

PLATE 102 Title page from the first in a series of deluxe editions published by Carl Hanser Verlag.
Diotima type with hand-lettered title by Zapf.

HERMANN ZAPF
& His Design Philosophy

Selected Articles and Lectures on Calligraphy

and Contemporary Developments in Type Design,

with Illustrations and Bibliographical Notes,

and a Complete List of His Typefaces

Introduction by Carl Zahn

SOCIETY OF TYPOGRAPHIC ARTS
CHICAGO

PLATE 103 Title page for a compilation of essays by Zapf, set in Zapf Renaissance Roman. Balanced asymmetry.

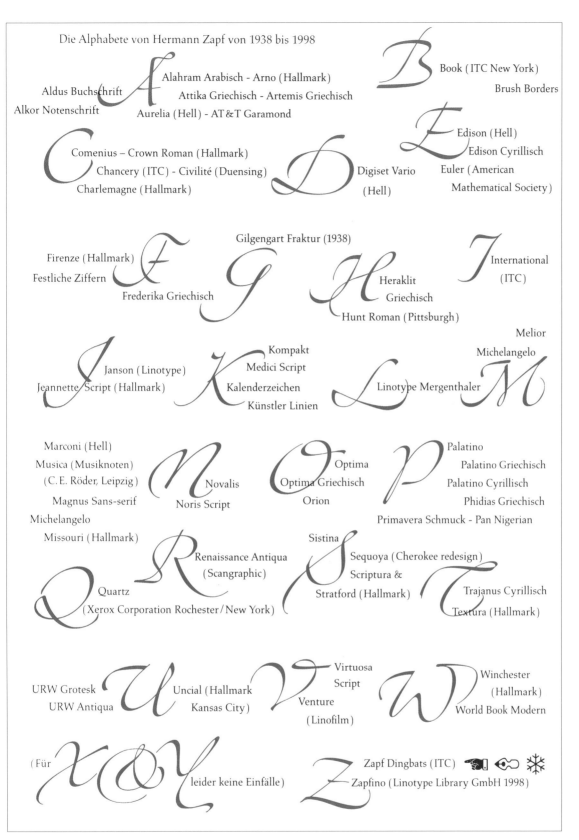

Die Alphabete von Hermann Zapf von 1938 bis 1998

Aldus Buchschrift
Alkor Notenschrift

A Alahram Arabisch - Arno (Hallmark)
Attika Griechisch - Artemis Griechisch
Aurelia (Hell) - AT&T Garamond

B Book (ITC New York)
Brush Borders

C Comenius – Crown Roman (Hallmark)
Chancery (ITC) - Civilité (Duensing)
Charlemagne (Hallmark)

D Digiset Vario
(Hell)

E Edison (Hell)
Edison Cyrillisch
Euler (American
Mathematical Society)

Firenze (Hallmark)
Festliche Ziffern

F Frederika Griechisch

Gilgengart Fraktur (1938)

G

H Heraklit
Griechisch
Hunt Roman (Pittsburgh)

I International
(ITC)

J Janson (Linotype)
Jeannette Script (Hallmark)

K Kompakt
Medici Script
Kalenderzeichen
Künstler Linien

L Linotype Mergenthaler

Melior
Michelangelo

M

Marconi (Hell)
Musica (Musiknoten)
(C. E. Röder, Leipzig)
Magnus Sans-serif
Michelangelo
Missouri (Hallmark)

N Novalis
Noris Script

O Optima
Optima Griechisch
Orion

P Palatino
Palatino Griechisch
Palatino Cyrillisch
Phidias Griechisch
Primavera Schmuck - Pan Nigerian

Q Quartz
(Xerox Corporation Rochester / New York)

R Renaissance Antiqua
(Scangraphic)

Sistina

S Sequoya (Cherokee redesign)
Scriptura &
Stratford (Hallmark)

T Trajanus Cyrillisch
Textura (Hallmark)

URW Grotesk
URW Antiqua

U Uncial (Hallmark
Kansas City)

V Virtuosa
Script
Venture
(Linofilm)

W Winchester
(Hallmark)
World Book Modern

(Für

X&Y leider keine Einfälle)

Z Zapf Dingbats (ITC)
Zapfino (Linotype Library GmbH 1998)

PLATE 104 A list of Zapf typefaces, set in Aldus with Zapfino initials, printed for Zapf's eightieth birthday.

BIBLIOGRAPHY

DANIEL BERKELEY UPDIKE

Hutner, Martin. *The Merrymount Press*. New York: The Grolier Club, 1983.

Morison, et al. *Updike: An American Printer*. New York: American Institute of Graphic Arts, 1947.

Smith, Julian Pearce. *Notes on the Merrymount Press and its Work*. Cambridge: Harvard University Press, 1934.

BRUCE ROGERS

Blumenthal, Joseph. *Bruce Rogers: A Life in Letters (1870-1957)*. Austin: W. Thomas Taylor, 1989.

Rogers, Bruce. *Paragraphs on Printing*. New York: William E. Rudge's Sons, 1943.

Warde, Frederic. *Bruce Rogers, Designer of Books*. Cambridge: Harvard University Press, 1972.

JOSEPH BLUMENTHAL

Blumenthal, Joseph. *The Spiral Press Through Four Decades: An Exhibition of Books and Ephemera*. New York: The Typophiles, 1957.

Cronenwett, Philip N. *The Spiral Press (1926-1971): A Bibliographical Checklist*. New York: The American Printing History Association, 2002.

STANLEY MORISON

Barker, Nicholas. *Stanley Morison*. Cambridge: Harvard University Press, 1972.

Morison, Stanley. *A Tally of Types*. Cambridge, England: privately printed, 1953.

FRANCIS MEYNELL

Dreyfus, John. *A History of The Nonesuch Press*. London: The Nonesuch Press, 1981.

Meynell, Francis. *My Lives*. New York: Random House, 1971.

GIOVANNI MARDERSTEIG

Barr, John. *The Officina Bodoni: Montagnola, Verona*. London: The British Library, 1978.

Schmoller, Hans. *The Officina Bodoni*. Verona: Edizioni Valdonega, 1980.

JAN VAN KRIMPEN

Dreyfus, John. *The Work of Jan van Krimpen: An Illustrated Record in Honor of his Sixtieth Birthday*. London: Sylvan Press, 1952.

Van Krimpen, Jan. *On Designing and Devising Type*. New York: The Typophiles, 1957.

JAN TSCHICHOLD

Klemke, Werner, ed. *Jan Tschichold: Leben und Werk des Typographen*. Dresden: Verlag der Kunst, 1977.

McLean, Ruari. *Jan Tschichold: Typographer*. Boston: David R. Godine, 1975.

Tschichold, Jan. *Designing Books*. New York: Wittenborn, Schultz, Inc., 1951.

Tschichold, Jan. *Schriften 1925--1974*. 2 volumes. Berlin: Brinkmann & Bose, 1991.

MAX CAFLISCH

Berlincourt, et al. *Max Caflisch: Typographica Practica*. Hamburg: Maximilian Gesellschaft, 1988.

GOTTHARD DE BEAUCLAIR

Fischer, Gert and Richter, Heinz, eds. *Gotthard de Beauclair: Buchgestalter/Lyriker/Verlager, 1907–1992. Leben und Werk*. Siegburg: Rheinlandia Verlag, 1996.

Kelly, Jerry. *Gotthard de Beauclair*. New York: The Grolier Club, 2007.

Schmoller, Hans. *Gotthard de Beauclair: Modern German Book Design*. London: Monotype House, 1960.

HERMANN ZAPF

Zahn, Carl. *Hermann Zapf & His Design Philosophy*. Chicago: Society of Typographic Arts, 1987.

Zapf, Hermann. *About Alphabets*. Revised edition. Cambridge: MIT Press, 1970.

Zapf, Hermann. *Hora Fugit – Carpe Diem: Ein Arbeitsbericht*. Hamburg: Maximilian Gesellschaft, 1984.

GENERAL

Blumenthal, Joseph. *The Art of the Printed Book*. New York: The Pierpont Morgan Library, 1972.

Blumenthal, Joseph. *The Printed Book in America*. Boston: David R. Godine, 1977.

Carter, Sebastian. *Twentieth Century Type Designers*. London: Trefoil, 1987.

Day, Kenneth, ed. *Book Typography 1815–1965*. Chicago: The University of Chicago Press, 1966.

Hutner, Martin and Kelly, Jerry. *A Century for the Century: Fine Printed Books from 1900 to 1999*. Revised edition published by David R. Godine, . Boston: David R. Godine, 2004.

Kelly, Jerry. *German Fine Printing 1948-1988*. New York: The Grolier Club, 1991.

Morison, Stanley and Simon, Oliver, eds. *The Fleuron*. 7 vols. London: The Fleuron [vols. 1–4], and Cambridge: Cambridge University Press [vols. 5–7], 1923–1930.

BIBLIOGRAPHY   Morison, Stanley and Kenneth Day. *The Typographic Book*. London: Ernest Benn, 1963.

Randle, John and Randle, Rosalind eds. *Matrix: A Review for Printers and Bibliophiles*. No. 1 (1981) through 28 (2009). Leominster: The Whittington Press.

Schauer, Georg Kurt. *Deutsche Buchkkunst 1890 bis 1960*. Hamburg: Maximilian Gesellschaft, 1963.

INDEX

NOTE: Page numbers in *italics* indicate figures.

About Alphabets (Zapf), 160, *162*
Adobe Systems, 55
Aesop's Fables, ix, *xi*, 20, 130
Albertus typeface, 141
Aldine typeface, 74
Aldrich, Thomas Bailey, 23
Aldus typeface, 142, 143, *149*, 158, 160–61
allusive typography, 20, 22, 38, 71, 102, 129–30
Alphabetum Romanum (Feliciano), 87–88, *95*
Amor und Psyche (Apuleius), 145, *154*
ampersands, *125*
Amyntas (Tasso), 160, 161, *169*
Antigone Greek typeface, 102, *111*
Apuleius, Lucius, 145, *154*
Armitage, Merle, xiii
Arrighi calligraphy, 86
Arrighi typeface, *68*, 85, 86
Ars Librorum, 143–44, *154*
Arts and Crafts movement, 3, 6
    See also Morris, William
Ashcan School, 39, 41
Ashendene Press, 57
asymmetric typography, *xv*, 115, 116, 130, 170–71

Bach, Johann Sebastian, *167*
Balzac typeface, 142
Baskerville typeface, 40–41, 57, 59, *61*, 87, 102, 160
Baskin, Leonard, 39, 41–42
Bauhaus style, xiii, 104, 116, 129
Bayer, Herbert, xiii
Beauclair, G. de. *See* de Beauclair, Gotthard
Beilenson, Peter, 37
Bell, John, 57, 58, *63*
Bell, Richard Anning, 4
Bell typeface, *5*, 57, 158
Bembo, Pietro, 74, 86
Bembo typeface, 57, 59, 87, 117, 130, *135*, 141, 158, 160
Benn, Ernest, 42
Bernhard typeface, xv
Bianchi, John, 4
Bible
    de Beauclair's design of, 143, *149*
    Mardersteig's design of, *97*
    Meynell's design of, 73, *76*
    Rogers's design of, 20, 21, *26*
    Van Krimpen's design of, 21, *108*, *113*
    Zapf's design of, 145, 160, *168*
Bill, Max, 115
Blado typeface, *64*, *81*
Blake, Stephenson, 57
Blake, William, 73
Blecher, Wilfried, 143

Blumenthal, Joseph, xv, 37–42, *43–53*
    design of *Aesop's Fables* by, ix, *xi*
    Emerson typeface of, 39–40, 42, 55, 86
    Morison and, 74
    portrait of, *36*
    Rogers and, 22
    Updike and, 7, 8
    Van Krimpen and, *103*
Bodoni, Giambattista, 85
Bodoni typeface, 85, 86, 130
Böhmer, Gunther, 84, *90–91*
Bonnard, Pierre, 85
Book of Common Prayer, 3–6, 17
Bowles, Joseph M., 19
Bremer Presse, 39–40
Breuer, Marcel, vii
Breviarum Romanum, *61*
Brown, Harold, 3
Bucolica (Virgil), 159, *164–66*
Bulmer typeface, 40–41, *47*, *53*
Burns & Oates publishers, 42, 56, 59, *61*, 71

Caflisch, Max, xv, 129–31, *132–39*
    portrait of, *128*
    Tschichold and, 118–19, 130
    typefaces of, 55
    writings of, 130, *138*
Calder, Alexander, 41, *47*
calligraphy, 71, 141
    on bindings, 144
    Koch and, 131
    Morison and, 58
    typefaces based on, 39, 86, 142, 158–59
    Van Krimpen and, 101, 104
    Zapf and, 145, 153, 158, 160
    See also typography
Cambridge University Press, 42
    Lewis at, 56
    Morison and, 57, *60*
    Tally of Types for, *67*
Cancelleresca Bastarda typeface, 102, *106*
Carter, Sebastian, 57
Caslon typeface, *11*, 102
    adaptations of, 71
    Tschichold and, 117, *123*
Centaur typeface, ix, 21, 55, 87, *99*, *122*, *133*
Cervantes, Miguel de, 159
Chirico, Giorgio de, 144
Chiswick Press, 7
Clarke, Bert, 21
Clarke & Way Press, 21, 22
Cleland, T. M., *5*, 37, 38
Cloister Press, 56
Coleridge, Samuel, *68*

Colish, A., 21, 37
Columna typeface, 55, 130, *137*
Cook, Howard, 39
Cranach Presse, 41, *164*
Crashaw, Richard, 102
Curwen Press, 103

D'Annunzio, Gabriele, 85, 86, *90–91*, 130
Dante typeface, xiv, 55, 86, 87, 89, *139*
de Beauclair, Gotthard, xv, xvi, 129, 141–45, *146–55*
    Koch and, 131, 141
    portrait of, *140*
    typefaces of, 55
    Zapf and, 131, 142, 145, 160
Delitsch, Hermann, 115
de Marinis, Tammaro, 87
Demos typeface, 130
de Tournes, Jean, x–xi, *xii*, 20
De Vinne Press, 7, 8
Diebenkorn, Richard, vii
Diehl, Edith, 21
digital-type generation, viii, xvi, 158, 160
Diotima typeface, 141, 142, 160, 161, *169*
Donne, John
    Paradoxes and Problemes by, ix, *x*
    poems of, *xvi*, 72, 103
Doves Press, 7, 57, 85
Dürer, Albrecht, 20, *28*
Dwiggins, W. A., xiii, 5, 12, 37

Eakins, Thomas, vii
Ecclesiastes, 26–27, *113*
Edition de Beauclair, 143, 144
Emerson typeface, xv, 39–40, 42, 45, *51*, 55, 86
Emig, Hermann, 160, *166*
Engel, Ernst, 141
Enschedé printing house, 101–4, *107*, 113
Epictetus, 130, *134*
Euclid, 20, 22, *34*
Eve typeface. *See* Koch Antiqua typeface

Faber and Faber, 87
Fass, John, 3, 37, 38
Feliciano, Felice, 87–88
Fell types, ix, 59, 82
film posters, 117, *120*
The Fleuron (journal), 56, 58, 74, 103
Fleuron Publishing Society, 57
Fonatana typeface, xiv
Fontana typeface, xiv, 86
Fournier typeface, 55, 57, 59
Francis of Assisi, 87
Frasconi, Antonio, ix, *xi*, 39, 41
Friedlaender, Henri, 141–42
Frost, Robert, 20, 38, *43*, *45*, *50*
Futura typeface, xv

Gag, Wanda, 39
Ganzo, Emil, 39
Garamond typeface, 40, 102
    adaptation of, 143
    Caflisch's use of, 131, *134*
    de Beauclair's use of, 141, *148*
    Mardersteig's use of, 87
    Monotype's version of, 59
    Tschichold's use of, 118, *126*
    Zapf's use of, 160
Garnett, David, 71–72
Garnett, Porter, 103–4
Gilgengart typeface, 160
Gill, Eric, 41, 59, 71, *80*, 86
Gill Sans typeface, 57
Goebbels, Joseph, 115
Golden Cockerel Press, 41
Gollancz, Victor, 58
Goodhue, Bertram Grosvenor, 4
Goudy, Frederic W., 21, *30*, 37
Grabhorn brothers, 37
Granjon Arabesque typeface, 130, *138*
Greene, Belle DaCosta, 4
Griffo, Francesco, 86
Griffo typeface, xiv, 74, 86
Grolier Club, 20, 88
    The American Livre de Peintre of, 39, 41
    Champ Fleury, 20
    Fra Luca de Pacioli of, *xiv*
    Of the Just Shaping of Letters, 28
    retrospective of, 52
Gropius, Walter, 46
Grosz, George, 41

handset type, 6, 20, 21, 56–57, 85, 158, 160
    See also typography
Harbor Press, 37, 38
Harrassowitz, Otto, 161
Heraklit typeface, 143, 145, *149*
Hoell, Louis, 39
Hoffman, Felix, 142, *152*
Hoffman, George, 37, 38, 40
Hofmannsthal, Hugo von, 142
Homer
    Iliad, 101–3, *109*
    Odyssey, 20, 21, 33, 103
Homo Caelestis, 130, *135*
Horne, Herbert, 13
Houghton Mifflin, 3, 8, 19
Hudson, W. H., 73
Huebsch publishing company, 37
Humanists' Library, 5, 6
Hunter, Dard, 22

Iliad (Homer), 101–3, *109*
Illing, Werner, *121*

The Imprint (journal), 55, 59, 71
Imprint Society, 119
Insel Verlag, 14, 87, 141–45, *146–48*
intaglio engraving, viii
International Typeface Corporation, 85
Irving, Washington, 5

Janson typeface, 5, 142–43, *152–53*
Joanna typeface, 86
Johnston, Edward, 71
Johnston Underground Sans typeface, 71
Joyce, James, 37

Kauffer, Edward McKnight, 41
Kellner, Ernst, 141
Kelmscott Press, 3, 7, 85
   handset type at, 57
   pamphlet on, 130, *133*
   Rogers and, 19, *24*
kerns, viii
Kippenberg, Anton, 141
Kleukens, Friedrich Wilhelm, 141
Klingspor typefoundry, 131, 141
Koch Antiqua typeface, xv, *38*, 39
Koch, Rudolf, 39, 72
   blackletter typeface of, *78*
   de Beauclair and, 131, 141
   Van Krimpen and, 104
Kredel, Fritz, 141, 143, *151*, 157
Krimpen, J. van. *See* van Krimpen, Jan

Labé, Louise, xi, *xii*, 131
Lamb, Charles, 5, *10*
Landeck, Armin, 39
Lawrence, D. H., 73
Lawrence, T. E., 20
Léger, Fernand, 41
letterpress process, viii, xvi
Lewis, C. Day, *123*
Lewis, Walter, 56
Limited Editions Club, 73
   Caflisch and, 119
   Epictetus's *Discourses* of, 134
   Mardersteig and, 87, *93*, *96*, *99*
   More's *Utopia* of, 32
   Ovid's *Metamorphoses* of, 87, *99*
   Rogers and, 20
   Shakespeare series of, 22
   Van Krimpen and, 101
Linotype Granjon typeface, 21
Linotype machines, xvii
lithography, viii, 85, 144
   See also letterpress
livres d'artiste, 41, 143
Loerke, Oskar, 160
Lutetia typeface, 21, 38–40, *44*, 55, 79, 101, *107*, 113

influence of, 103–4
   open capitals for, 103

Macy, George, 72, 73
Maillol, Aristide, 41, *164*
Manuale Typographicum (Zapf), 157, 160
Manutius, Aldo, 86
Marchbanks Press, 21, 37
Marconi typeface, 130
Mardersteig, Giovanni, xv, 85–88, *89–99*
   allusive typography and, 130
   Morison and, 74, 88
   portrait of, *84*
   typefaces of, xiv, 55, 86, 87
   Updike and, 7, 8
   Van Krimpen and, 103
   Zapf and, 158, 159, 161
Mardersteig, Martino (Giovanni's son), 88
Marinis, Tammaro de, 87
Marsh, Reginald, 39
Martin, Noel, 116
Matisse, Henri, 41
McCutcheon, John, 19
McLean, Ruari, 115
Melior typeface, 157
Merker, Kim, xvi
Merrymount Press, 4–7, 37
   ephemera from, 6, *14*
   handset type at, 57
   promotional booklet for, 3, *9*
   typefaces for, 5, 55
Meynell, Alice (FM's mother), 71
Meynell, Francis, x, xv, 71–74, *75–83*
   allusive typography of, 20, 38, 71, 129
   autobiography of, 73
   borders used by, x–xi, *xii*
   design of *Paradoxes and Problemes* by, ix, *x*
   Morison and, 56, 59, 74
   Nonesuch Press and, 59, 72
   Pelican Press and, 56, 69, 71
   poetry of, 73
   Rogers and, 71
   typefaces of, 55
   Typography by, 71, *75*
   Van Krimpen and, 104
   Zapf and, 158
Meynell, Gerard (FM's cousin), 56, 59, 71
Meynell, Vera (FM's wife), 72
Meynell, Wilfrid (FM's father), 56, 59, 71
Michelangelo typeface, 41, *148*
Mies van der Rohe, Ludwig, vii
Mondadori, Arnoldo, 86
Monotype Corporation, xiv, xvii, 40, 102, *132*
   Dante and, 86
   Goudy and, 21, *30*
   handset type and, 57

INDEX

Montallegro typeface, 5, *13*
Moreas, Jean, 144
Morgan, J. P., Jr., 4
Morison, Stanley, xiv, xv, 55–59, *60–69*
    allusive typography of, 20, 38, 129
    design of *Fra Luca de Pacioli* by, *xiv*
    handset type and, 56–57
    Mardersteig and, 85, 88
    Meynell and, 56, 59, 74
    at Monotype Corporation, 40, 57
    portrait of, *54*
    Times New Roman typeface of, 5, 55
    Updike and, 7, 8, 55
    Van Krimpen and, 102
Morris, William, 3, 6, 19
    allusive typography of, 38
    pamphlet on, 130, *133*
    Zapf on, 159
Mountjoye typeface, 5
Munder, Norman T. A., 21

Nash, John Henry, 37
Nash, Paul, 41, 72
Neuland typeface, 72
Newdigate, Bernard, 57
New Directions, 87
Nonesuch Press, 41, 72–73
    Compendium series of, 73
    founding of, 59, 72
    Genesis of, 72, *76*
    sample title pages of, *77–82*
    Shakespeare edition of, 55

Odyssey (Homer), 20, 21, *33*, 103
Oehms, Ludwig, 160
Offenbach Werkstatt, 131, 141
Officina Bodoni, xiv, 74, 85–88
    samples from, *92, 94, 95, 97, 98*
    See also Mardersteig, Giovanni
Offizin Haag-Drugulin, 141
offset printing, viii, xvi, 88, 158
On Designing and Devising Type (Van Krimpen), 102
On the Dedication of American Churches, 3, 4
Open Kapitalen typeface, 102, 103, *105*
Optima typeface, 55, 130, 142, 157, *160, 162, 163*
Ovid's *Metamorphoses*, 87, *99*
Oxford University Press, xi, *xiii*, 20

Pacioli, Luca de, *98*
Pacioli typeface, xiv, 86
Palatino typeface, 55, 141, 157, *168*
    Aldus and, 142, 160–61
    first book in, 142, 145, *150*
Pantheon Books, 87
Pegasus Press, 101
Pegasus typeface, 141

Pelican Press, 56, 69, 71, *75*
Penguin Books, 116, *123, 124, 127*
Perpetua typeface, 40, 52, 59, *67, 80*, 86
Petrarch, Francesco, 5, *13*, 20
phototypesetting, vii–viii, 103, 142, 160
Picasso, Pablo, 41
Pierrot's Verses, 5, *12*
Pingel, Willy, 143, 160
Plantin Light typeface, 55
Plato, 20, 86
Poe, Edgar Allan, 39, *44*
Poeschel, Carl Ernst, 141
Poliphili publishing house, 87
Poliphilus typeface, 57
Pollock, Jackson, vii
Pope, Alexander, 82
posters, by Tschichold, 117, *120*
Post, Herbert, 141
Printing Types, 7–8
Propyläen publishing house, 144

Rand, Paul, 39
Renaissance typeface, 55
Riezler, Walter, 159
Rilke, Rainer Maria, 142, 144, *148, 150*
Riverside Press, 3, 4, 8, 19–20, 22, *23–27*
Rogers, Bruce, ix–xv, *ix, xii–xiv*, 19–22, *23–35*, 57, 118
    allusive typography of, 20, 22, 38, 129
    Blumenthal on, 22
    Centaur typeface of, 21, 55, 86
    Meynell on, 71
    portrait of, *18*
    at Riverside Press, 3, 8, 19–20, *23–27*
    at Rudge's press, 7, 21, 37
    Van Krimpen and, 103
    Zapf and, 158
Rollins, Carl, 21
Romanée typeface, 101–2
Romney Street Press, 71
Romulus typeface, 55, 103
Ronsard, Pierre de, xi, *xii*, 20
Rouault, Georges, 41
Rousseau, Jean-Jacques, *80*
Rowfant Club, 22
Rubáiyát of Omar Khayyám, 103, *106*
Rudge, William Edwin, 7, 21, 37
Ruzicka, Rudolph, 5, *11*

Sabon typeface, 55, 142, 143, *151*
Sachs, Nelly, 159, 161
Sappho Revocata, 102, *111*
Sargent, John Singer, vii
Schauer, Georg Kurt, 142
Schmoller, Hans, 88
Schwabacher typeface, 143
Schwabe publishing house, 118

Shahn, Ben, 39, 41, *48*
Shakespeare Head Press, 57
Shakespeare, William, 22
    Birkhäuser edition of, 116–17
    Nonesuch edition of, 55, 73
Sichowsky, Richard von, 141
Sistina typeface, 41, *49*
Slimbach, Robert, 55
Spectrum typeface, 55, 102
Spiral Press, 7, 22, 37–42, *43–53*
Sporer, Eugen, 141
Stamperia Valdonega, 7, 74, 87–88
Standard, Paul, 157
Steiner-Prag, Hugo, 115
Stempel typefoundry, 55, *125*, 142, *143*, 145
Stone, Reynolds, 41, 58, *62, 67, 80*, 124
Stresow, Gustav, 42, 141
Suhrkamp Verlag, 159, *164–65*

Tasso, Torquato, 160, 161, *169*
Taylor & Taylor, 37
Tennyson, Alfred Lord, 72, *81*
Tiemann, Walter, 115, 141
Times New Roman typeface, 5, 55, 57, 59, 131
Tory, Geoffroy, 26–27, *29*
Tournes, Jean de, x–xi, *xii*, 20
Trajanus Presse, 142–44, *150–53*
Tristan und Isolde, 143, *151*
Trump typeface, 141, 158, 160
Tschichold, Jan, x, xiii–xv, 115–19, *120–27*, 125
    Bauhaus and, 129
    Caflisch and, 118–19, 130
    portrait of, *114*
    Sabon typeface of, 55
    Van Krimpen and, 104
    writings of, *xv*, 115, *122, 125*
    Zapt and, 158, 159
Typographic Variations (Zapf), 157, 160, *163, 167*
Typographische Gestaltung (Tschichold), 115, 116, 117
typography
    allusive, 20, 22, 38, 71, 102, 129–30
    asymmetric, *xv*, 115, 116, 130, *170–71*
    calligraphy and, 39, 86, 142, 158–59
    digital, viii, xvi, 158, 160
    handset, 6, 20, 21, 56–57, 85, 158, 160
    phototypesetting and, vii–viii, 103, 142, 160
    See also individual typefaces
Typography (Meynell), 71, 75

Updike, Daniel Berkeley, xv, 3–8, *9–17*, 37, 118
    allusive typography of, 20, 22, 38, 129
    handset type and, 57
    Morison and, 7, 8, 55, 74
    portrait of, *2*
    typefaces of, 55

Van Krimpen and, 103
Zapf and, 158
Utopia (More), 20, *32*
Utopolis (Illing), *121*

van Krimpen, Jan, xiv, xv, 101–4, *105–13*
    allusive typography and, 130
    Bible designs of, 21, *108, 113*
    calligraphy of, 101, 104
    Mardersteig and, 103
    Morison and, 102
    portrait of, *100*
    typefaces of, 21, 38–40, 55, 101–4
    Zapt and, 158
Vasetta, Mauro, 85
Venetian Printers, 30
Vicenza typeface, 85
Village Press, 7
Villon, François, *112*
Virchow, Rudolf, *136*
Virgil, 159, *164–66*
von Hofmannsthal, Hugo, 142
von Sichowsky, Richard, 141

Walbaum typeface, *136*, 141, 143–44, 160
Walker, Emery, 21
Warde, Frederic, 37, *68*, 85, 86
Watenphul, Max Pfeiffer, 144
Way, David, 21
Way & Williams publishers, 19
Weber, Max (artist), 41
Weiss typeface, 41, *137*
Westminster Press, 71
Wiegand, Willy, 39
Wiemeler, Ignatz, 141
Wilkes, Walter, 143
Willberg, Peter, 116
Wolff, Kurt, 85, 87
Wolpe, Berthold, 141
Wright, Frank Lloyd, vii

Zapf, Hermann, xv, xvi, 129, 141, 157–61, *162–71*
    Bible design of, 145, 160, *168*
    Blumenthal and, 39
    calligraphy and, 145, 153, 158, 160
    de Beauclair and, 131, 142, 145, 160
    Mardersteig and, 158, 159, 161
    portrait of, *156*
    typefaces of, 41, *49*, 55, 157, *171*
    Updike and, 158
    Van Krimpen and, 104
    writings by, 142, 145, 157, 159–60, *162, 163*
Zapf–von Hesse, Gudrun, 160, 161
Zeno typeface, xiv, 86, *97*

EDITORIAL & PRODUCTION BY MOLLY CORT.
PRINTED BY THE ROCHESTER INSTITUTE OF TECHNOLOGY
PRINTING APPLICATIONS LABORATORY.
BOUND BY HOSTER BINDERY, INC.
SET IN HERMANN ZAPF'S ALDUS TYPE.
DESIGN & TYPOGRAPHY BY JERRY KELLY.

THIS BOOK IS MADE POSSIBLE, IN PART, BY SUPPORT FROM THE
BOWER FAMILY PUBLICATION FUND AT RIT.